WE DON'T KILL SNAKES WHERE WE COME FROM

We Don't Kill Snakes Where We Come From

Two Years in a Greek Village

John Levy

Querencia Books
El Paso & Tucson

Cover art by Leslie Buchanan

Cover design by Lisa Stotska

Frontispiece art by Leslie Buchanan

Map by Leslie Buchanan

Copyright © 1994 by John Levy

Querrencia Books
8987 E. Tanque Verde Road, #111
Tucson, Arizona 85749

First Printing, 1994

ISBN 1-882168-02-X (pbk)

Library of Congress Catalog Card Number: 92-81744

Printed on acid-free paper

For Leslie Buchanan

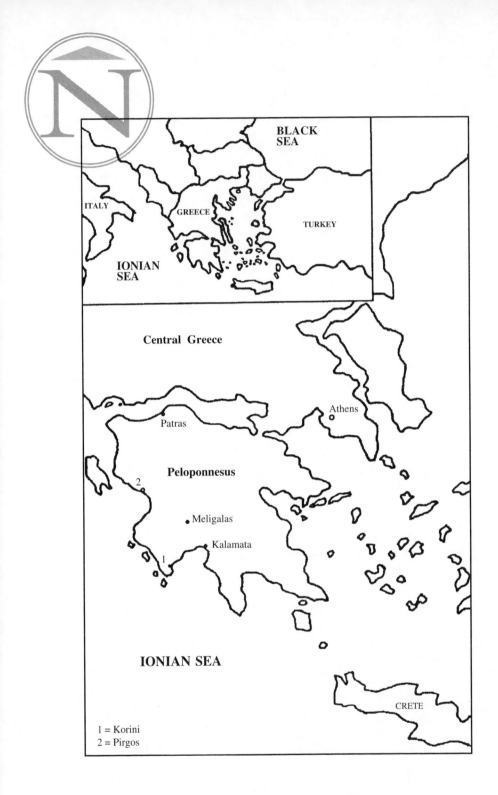

Central Greece

Patras

Peloponnesus

Meligalas

Kalamata

BLACK
SEA

ITALY

GREECE

TURKEY

IONIAN
SEA

Athens

IONIAN SEA

CRETE

1 = Korini
2 = Pirgos

CONTENTS

ACKNOWLEDGMENTS

Some of the poems and prose in this book first appeared in the following magazines: *Infolio* (England), *Longhouse* (U.S.), *Shearsman* (England), *Smoot Drive Press* (U.S.), *The Southeastern Review* (Greece) and *Sow's Ear* (England). Ten Crow press (U.S.) published five of the poems in *A Larger Canvas,* a limited edition book with linoleum engravings by Ed Cain.

A special thanks to Leslie Buchanan, whose responses have guided me as I edited and revised this book. I could not have written the book without her. In addition, I am grateful for her permission to quote her letters. My thanks to Vassilis Zambaras, who has helped me with the book from its beginning through its completion; his advice has been invaluable, and I also thank him for suggesting the book's title. Robert Bulechek also helped me countless times, and I gratefully acknowledge his patient, generous assistance in designing the book for publication. I am also indebted to Ed Cain, Tree Swenson, and Lisa Stotska for help with book design decisions. And I wish to thank the people who read the book at various stages and helped me edit it: Zoe Levy, I. Harrison Levy, James L. Weil, David Miller, Robert Lax, Ted Schneyer, Toni Massaro, Marcia Lindley, Ed Cain, Adrienne Bridgewater, and Alex Anderson.

PREFACE

This book combines notes and poems from my journal, several passages from my letters to family and friends, Leslie Buchanan's letters to her family, and a handful of quotations from my students.

We left Greece in August 1985. Since then I have continued work on this book, revising the prose and usually leaving the poems as I wrote them while in Greece. I have changed the names of several people in the book.

John Levy
Tucson, Arizona
September 1993

FACTUAL BACKGROUND

The Zambaras Story

Vassilis Zambaras was born in 1944 in Revmatia, a small Greek village. When he was four he moved to Raymond, Washington with his parents. In 1959 Vassilis returned with his parents to Meligalas, a village near Revmatia. For the next 16 years Vassilis travelled between Greece and the U.S.

I met Vassilis in 1970 at a writer's conference in Colorado. We share an interest in poetry and read many of the same poets. His own poems, written in English, show a sharply focused intelligence. Sometimes no longer than four words, and in the last ten years never longer than half a page, the poems usually have at least a couple of puns, may be humorous, may question or declare, celebrate or scorn, but always the sounds make clear the syllable-by-syllable care with which Vassilis hears words as he creates poems.

Vassilis settled in Greece in 1975. I visited him for a week in January 1977. He and his mother treated me with incredible hospitality. In the village there were chickens in the street, tile-roofed white houses, villagers leading donkeys, and just a minute's walk from the village, a silence and peacefulness in the countryside. I fell in love with Meligalas. In 1978 Vassilis began a language school in the village. When I visited in 1982, he was married to Eleni and she was pregnant with their second child. Vassilis asked me to be godfather. He explained the importance of being a godparent in Greece: the godfather baptizes the child and assumes certain responsibilities if the father dies before the child grows up. I understood the honor of being asked.

I wanted to live in Meligalas during my godchild's first years, so once back in Arizona I sent Vassilis the required documents for a work permit. He submitted the papers to bureaucrats in Athens. Meanwhile, I had met my future wife, Leslie Buchanan, a painter who was finishing nursing school. She had dreamed of living in Greece ever since she had read Kazantzakis and had also hoped to devote some time solely to painting. We decided to go to Greece: I would teach English and she would paint.

The Village

In Leslie's first letter home from Meligalas she wrote that in some ways the village resembled Tucson because of the nearby mountains and the vegetation, "except that there aren't all the cactus, only prickly pears. There are olive groves, cypress trees and figs and mulberries. It is moister, though, so grapes grow all over the village, and people have beautiful lush gardens."

Meligalas is an inland village in the southern Peloponnesus. Its population of about 1,200 makes it the largest village in the vicinity. Its main businesses are olives, figs, and currants. It has become the commercial center of the area because of its government services, including banks, revenue offices, and social service offices.

Politics Politics Politics

The first time I visited Greece I heard two men having what sounded like a violent argument. Vassilis told me they were *agreeing* about a politician's recent speech. One reason for passionate conversations about politics is that the parties are very different from each other. Another reason is that Greeks like conversations with flair and drama.

Twentieth century Greece has experienced kings, dictators, democracies, coups d'etat, an occupation, and civil wars. There were 44 political parties contesting 250 parliamentary seats in the 1950 elections. In the 1963 election there were only four political parties. The shifting coalitions between parties, combined with frequent elections, created political instability, which a small group of army officers took advantage of by executing a coup in 1967. These officers suspended policitcal parties and ruled until they became so hated that they were overthrown by another military group, which reestablished civilian parliamentary democracy. In the resulting election, the New Democracy Party (ND), center right and pro-Western, prevailed while the Panhellenic Socialist Movement (PASOK), a new center left party led by Andreas Papandreou, received about 13% of the vote. In 1977 ND won again, but in 1981 PASOK won. The other major party was the pro-Moscow Communist party. PASOK governed while Leslie and I lived in Greece.

A family usually agrees on a political party, and this affiliation is known in the community. Vassilis led the local PASOK group for several years before 1981. Because of his visibility as a political leader, his school's enrollment shrank from over 100 to about 40. He finally had to resign from the political position so he could continue to support his family with the school.

Teaching in Kalamata

Kalamata is a half-hour's drive from Meligalas. In 1983 Kalamata had popular beaches, a busy harbor, and a population of over 40,000. The first year I taught at three private English schools. My students were intermediate or advanced and usually between the ages of 12 and 18. I worked a few hours a week at two schools and almost full-time at Roula Christaki's school. The second year I taught full-time for Roula.

After We Left

On September 13, 1986, Kalamata was hit by a strong earthquake. At least 19 people were killed and 3,000 injured. The quake damaged about 70% of the buildings and almost levelled a nearby village. Aftershocks on September 15 injured more than 30 people and damaged more buildings. From what I could discover from students' letters, no one I'd taught or known was killed or severely injured. Some of my students' homes, however, were demolished. Many families moved away from Kalamata, at least for a year or more.

I visited Greece in January 1991. Kalamata showed signs of having been partly destroyed. Some buildings were surrounded by scaffolding, and some lots on which buildings had collapsed were empty or had a scattering of rubble. But many old buildings had been restored and new ones completed; the town seemed to have mostly recovered from the catastrophe.

WE DON'T KILL SNAKES WHERE WE COME FROM

1983

Arrived in Meligalas this afternoon.

Not afraid of strangers, my blue-eyed blond godson, four months old, smiles at Leslie and me. Everyone calls him "Baby" (infants are called that until they are baptized).

Efiniki, Baby's two-and-a-half-year-old sister, has curly brown hair and knows she's a beauty. She has a repertoire that includes partly learned songs in English, such as "Jingle Bells," and perfectly delivered Greek curses.

Vassilis's mother lives in the house too. In her room, on top of an armoire, stand several framed reproductions of saints with small electric bulbs glowing in front of them. She lived in Raymond, Washington for more than ten years but forgot most of the English she learned. She uses Vassilis as a translator first to welcome us and then to tell us that we should sleep in her double bed and she can sleep on the small couch in her room. We suggest we could sleep in our sleeping bags on her floor, assuring her we'd be comfortable, but she insists.

Eleni prepares a feast. Then, after the children and Vassilis's mother go to bed, Vassilis translates for Eleni as we continue to talk around the kitchen table. We learn of the disagreement over Baby's name.

Vassilis created the name Efiniki, combining the first part of his mother's name with the name of Efiniki's godfather, Nikos. Vassilis says Baby should be named Anastasios (Tasso, for short) after Vassilis's father. Greek tradition mandates the first son be named after the father's father. Eleni argues that since Vassilis named Efiniki, she should name Baby. She favors any name but Anastasios. Vassilis counters that, although she has a good point, tradition must be honored. As godfather, it seems I have a role in resolving this dispute. I side with Eleni, although we all agree we don't have to settle this tonight. Baby doesn't need a name until his baptism, which won't be for eight or nine months.

August 20

Finally found a vacant house. We first go meet Christos, a man in his mid-70s who is the owner's brother-in-law. (The owner and his wife spend most of their time in Australia where their children live.) Vassilis translates for us as we walk toward the house.

On one of the last unpaved roads in Meligalas and standing by itself on a slope, the shabby little two story house fits in well with the run-down houses near it. Inside the front door are two cobwebbed rooms on either side of a hall. One room was once hot pink, the other light blue; grime dims the colors now.

The grey wooden floor planks are buried under dirt, curled hardened millipedes, splinters from the rooms' shattered windows, cigarette butts, and discards such as a tattered grade school workbook, a rusted hair spray can without its nozzle and a few balled-up stiff socks. Opening the back door, we walk out onto a large terrace with a kitchen to one side.

We know we want the house as soon as we go out on the terrace and look down into a valley of olive groves, fields, meadows, cypresses, and a handful of villages. A train track brings a four car train into the view, and from where we are the train appears toy-sized. In both directions the land extends a distance and then lifts into high mountain ranges.

The kitchen walls sport a black mildew plus a thick layer of grease near the counter and sink. Off to the side of the kitchen a tiny room with crumbling walls contains a discolored, seatless toilet that doesn't work. Eleni's brother, Theodoros, can fix it and install a shower.

Chickens noisily run and flap into the backyard as we descend the steps to the lower level of the house. They had been escaping the heat by gathering in the shade under the terrace.

We decide that the room on the lower level, beneath the kitchen, will be Leslie's studio because it has windows to the north and east. A big cellar is located under the main part of the house. As we open the cellar door a plump rat scratches across the floor and vanishes behind a stack of bricks. $39.00 a month. An unusually low rent.

The north side yard slants down in a weedy stretch the villagers use as a dump. A 6 ft. drop to this area makes the road's edge an ideal place to come with big (push them off) and little (hurl them off) items. The backyard is less accessible, though a path runs along its south edge and so it too has been bombarded with garbage.

August 25

The Fotopoulos family lives in a stone house near us. The mother, a stout widow, looks grim although she smiles whenever she sees us. Her two adult children live with her: Yiota, dark-haired, pretty, and cheerful, and a son who shepherds their flock of sheep and rides a frail, noisy motorbike.

Roula, the short, gap-toothed widow in the small stone house diagonally across from us, dresses all in black, including a black scarf over her hair. She keeps chickens in her backyard and releases them in the morning; they spend the day in our backyard.

Five days fixing up the house and we're about halfway through. The Meligalas glazier replaced our windows, which we keep open because of the heat. Two windows face the dirt road, one in our bedroom and one in the room I'll make my study. As we clean and paint these rooms an audience gathers outside. Most villagers stare about 15 minutes and then leave. Roula watches three hours a day, leaning on the sill, saying "o-*ray*-o" (the Greek word for "beautiful") every two minutes. She seems to be talking to herself as much as to us. Mrs. Fotopoulos joins her a few times a day and shouts the same word.

September 3

Last week I visited a man who owns an English language school in Kalamata. I told him my qualifications, but we mostly talked about his travels in the U.S. He hired me to teach several classes a week and asked me to come back today to discuss the job. But today, instead of talking about the classes, he wanted me to tell him about myself. I mentioned that I write poetry. He said he writes too.

"What do you write about," I asked.

"The burgen of life."

"The *burden* of life?" Last week he had proudly said he was a pessimist. I imagined that he wrote about life as a burden, perhaps about how to accept it.

"No, the *bargain* of life." He smiled.

Did he mean each person must make a bargain with God? But what could we offer? Praise for all that has been created? Kindness to all? The window behind the man let in daylight: the light seemed glorious.

"I take it all from an economic standpoint." He leaned

back in his swivel chair. And before I could think of anything to say he told me he couldn't afford to pay me 450 drachmas ($4.50) an hour, the standard hourly wage for a foreign English teacher in Kalamata. I refused 300. After I accepted 350, he grinned.

As I left, I looked up at his sign on the outside of the building. Below the school name is his name, followed by "U.C.S.B." I assumed the acronym stood for a Greek degree. Tonight I asked Vassilis about it. He told me that the letters are supposed to look like a degree and that Greeks assume the man has some kind of foreign degree in the English language. However, the letters are for "University of California at Santa Barbara." Then I remembered that last week this man told me that when he visited California he took a couple of classes but soon got bored and quit.

September 15

This morning, in front of the whitewashed stone house across from Vassilis's house, an old woman in a black dress and a thin old man were stomping grapes in a cart. It was hot and they were working hard. They smiled when I greeted them, and the woman handed me purple grapes and said something emphatically. An old man on the ground handed me another bunch and the woman gave me more. I had to use both hands to hold them all.

I went to Vassilis's house and asked him to come and translate.

"Excuse us," the old woman had said, "these grapes are a little squished. Come back tonight and we'll have better ones to give you."

September 16

Leslie and I walked over to Vassilis's house last night. The neighbors were stomping a new batch. With Vassilis translating, we asked if we could work with them.

This morning Leslie and I climbed into a fresh cartload of purple grapes. The sun hot, our feet bare, the grapes cool. The floor of the cart is covered by a plastic sheet, and the juice runs out of the cart in a rivulet that pours down through a straw basket (a strainer) into a big jug.

Leslie cried out in pain when she was stung in the foot by a bee that had been buried alive in the grapes. Soon I got stung in the foot too, then in the palm when I was moving grapes out of a corner. Leslie got stung on her soles twice more in our three hours of trodding.

October 8

Eleni's cousin met her future husband at a disco four months ago. Saturday night we drove with Vassilis and Eleni to the cousin's engagement ceremony in a nearby mountain village. Leslie and I were invited because I'm Baby's godfather, which makes us members of both Vassilis's and Eleni's families.

Couples seldom break engagements in Greece, although Vassilis says that the breaking of engagements is becoming more frequent because of the "Westernizing" influence. An engagement ceremony gives the families a chance to meet and begin a harmonious relationship. Also, the celebration makes public the engagement. At the typical engagement party the families dance to a record player turned up full volume so the village actually hears the rejoicing. But this ceremony was supposed to be subdued because the groom's mother had died recently.

The party began at the bride's parents' home at 7 p.m. We arrived on time to find the house almost empty. The bride's family arrived between 7:45 and 8:00. None of the groom's family had come yet. Vassilis explained the groom and his family usually show up late. He told us that he had kept Eleni waiting an hour so he wouldn't seem "overanxious."

The attractive 18-year-old bride, tall, shapely, fair-skinned, with long black hair and large brown eyes, glowed as she calmly welcomed guests and helped her mother with last-minute details. The guests, mostly older couples, were led into the hot pink "best room." Long tables had been arranged near three walls of the room. By 8:15 all of the bride's family were sitting at the tables talking and laughing. Like Eleni's parents, most of her cousins tend sheep and/or farm. One man in a plaid shirt had a green sprig of basil tucked behind his ear, and as he talked he'd frequently hold the basil near his nose. A few times he passed it to the men near him and they'd sniff it too.

A little after 8:15 the bride began to look nervous and humiliated. She stopped talking and all other conversations grew hushed. At 8:30 the wine was served and the room filled with talk and laughter again. As it neared 9:00 the guests, some already tipsy, became more animated. We all sneaked glances at both the door and the dejected girl in white.

At 9:05 the groom's party arrived. The groom, a tall, handsome young man, followed his family through the door-way, hurried over to the bride, and was deferential, even sheepish, as he whispered to her. She glowed again. They stood together in the center of the room beaming at each other and the priest stepped in front of them. Guests continued to greet each other as the ceremony began. The groom's father is a trim, good-looking man, about 55, with deep lines in his face that give him a severe appearance. He gazed somberly at the couple. The priest called him forward to perform the blessings of the rings.

The groom's father held the two rings, made the sign of the cross on the bride's and groom's foreheads, repeated this gesture many times before placing the groom's ring on the bride's hand and the bride's on the groom's hand. He solemnly said a vow, switched the rings back and forth as he recited the vow two more times, and then left the rings on the correct fingers. The priest uttered a few words, everyone kissed everyone else, and the bride and groom exchanged gifts with each other and then gave gifts to each other's families. The groom's father made a serious, thoughtful toast. Other people toasted the couple as the small glasses were filled with wine and emptied, filled and emptied again and again. The bride's family brought us pastries and Jordan almonds. Soon we were served lamb and potatoes along with salad and bread.

As we finished the main course a heavy man near us started making loud noises, which became recognizable as the beginning of a song. Almost half the guests, all from the bride's family, took up the folk song. Vassilis whispered that the man who had started singing was the bride's brother-in-law, a policeman in Athens. Impressed by his own voice, the policeman stood and performed. The groom's family kept their mouths firmly shut. Greeks have many rituals and beliefs about mourning; the widower obviously felt the singers showed no respect for his late wife. After the first song concluded, the policeman melodramatically began a solo. He looked around the room proudly as he sang. The groom's father's face, which had frozen into a tense mask, began to glisten with sweat.

The second song was ending when an old man on the other side of the room rose, earnestly addressed the whole room, and then spoke gently to the groom's father who nodded his thanks. Another old man across from Leslie and me, who had continued downing wine through the two songs, jumped up and turned to the groom's father. He started singing loudly and broke off to tell the groom's father that *nothing* can stop a man who wants to sing. The groom's father looked at him sternly, but the old man continued with renewed conviction. A minute later the bride's relatives joined the song, and the room was again divided between singers and stiff, quiet figures. Vassilis said softly it was as if the bride's family were telling the groom's family to "fuck off."

During all of this the engaged couple, seated next to the groom's father, silently stared straight ahead of them at the hot pink wall across the room.

The songs followed each other with no break. Finally Vassilis whispered that we should leave. It was 11:00 and we were the first to go.

On the drive back, Vassilis said the bride's mother had disapproved of the marriage but was finally persuaded to allow it. Everyone in both families knew of her opposition.

Poetics

like that chicken down there
who has scratched the earth clear
of weeds and debris
to find one thing fresh

October 24

Last night Vassilis and Eleni were supposed to visit after dinner. They arrived late and Vassilis explained that Meni, the metalworker, had died in an accident that afternoon and so they'd visited Meni's parents. Eleni went in to light a candle. Vassilis waited in the car.

Meni had his shop across from Vassilis's English school. A handsome young man, dark-haired, macho, who in the bright hot days wore no shirt, proud of his lean, muscular body. I'd see him on the street, or through his shop's dirty windows I'd sometimes make him out in the shadowy interior illuminated by sparks as he welded. The last time I saw him was the only time I thought we might become friends. Eleni's brother, Takis, had been Meni's apprentice for two years. As I walked by the shop, Takis shouted to me. Meni turned, said something to Takis, and then looked out at me with curiosity and a smile. I smiled back.

Meni had been in a nearby village talking to a friend who had a house next to a two-lane freeway. Meni got onto his motorcycle and, without looking back, pulled out onto the freeway as a truck sped around a bend behind him. He was killed instantly. Shocking news for Meligalas because of Meni's youth and popularity and also because his wife is pregnant.

We have had clear days for two months, but this morning we woke to see the village partially erased by a light mist. Usually people are out on the street in the early morning, and I exchange greetings with everyone. This morning I walked through the mist without seeing anyone.

At the bakery the baker's assistant, a tall, paunchy man in his late 20s, began sliding loaves into the oven using a wooden paddle with a 6 ft. long handle. The oven was empty and he slipped the first loaves in against the far wall. He kept a double-edged razor blade between his teeth and used it to stroke two long slits along the top of each loaf. Working fast, with precision and grace, he took pride in his skill. He had filled most of the oven when the door opened and a woman entered. She said a few words. I've been studying Greek and understood she was asking what time something would be. Then, from her tone, I realized she wanted to know about Meni's funeral. He took the razor blade out of his mouth and answered.

October 26

Before Meni's death Meligalas seemed a random collection of people. The lanky, grinning young guy sitting on a chair outside the furniture store where he works and where we bought our mattress, table, chairs. A heavy woman I see in her backyard near her flower garden. The mailman. The fat butcher in his stained apron. Roula. Mrs. Fotopoulos. Vassilis, Eleni. For two days the village has seemed unified; everyone, including Leslie and I, has been thinking about Meni.

November 16

Today I brought our car to Pirgos for a checkup. I found a *kaffaneia* (coffee shop) with clean tables, classical music, and a display case for pastries. I sat in the corner and read my Greek language book, doing vocabulary and grammar exercises. Two men near me argued about politics. Their voices rose and I recognized many more words than I did last month.

I moved to a smaller *kaffaneia* that played Gypsy music. There were three workmen, no businessmen or mothers with children like in the other *kaffaneia*. Three "travel" posters were tacked to the imitation wood paneling, each showing a bare-breasted woman with a caption identifying her nationality. Two British women pouted seductively. The American smiled, standing on a deserted beach and holding her blonde hair back from her face. Of course, no posters of bare-breasted Greek women.

Two little girls, one about five and the other about seven, came out of the kitchen and began to wander between the tables. The youngest girl sat down at a table by herself, smiled at me (because I was the only one who noticed her), and then stared at a shirtless man, a gold tooth in his grin as he talked to the other man at his table.

There was only the Gypsy music and quiet talk for about 15 minutes. Then two men at different tables started a discussion. Among the Greek words I recognized were "money," "Athens," "bases," and "America." I have heard this argument many times. The man in favor of PASOK said Greece should keep its distance from the U.S. and get rid of the base in Athens. The other man was arguing Greece should be close to the U.S. in order to get a lot of money in aid and military protection. The men had started the discussion sitting down, at their respective tables. Then both stood and started to shout. Soon one strode over and stood six inches from the other. The man backed against his table slammed his knuckles against a closed wooden backgammon set on the table as he made a point — the pieces inside the box rattled — then he slammed it with his knuckles a second time, a third, and the other man began to speak in a quiet, measured way.

I imagined scenes like this 2,400 years ago. The land of debates, of democracy.

November 28

You thwack olives off a tree with a stick because there are too many to pick by hand. First, you spread tarps under the tree. Most olives land on the tarps, though a few fly beyond. Yesterday Leslie and I helped Eleni's family harvest their olive trees. We drove Eleni, Baby, and Efiniki into the mountains and parked off the paved road. Vassilis has been up there since the day before yesterday. Eleni led us along a dirt path to the mountainside where her family owns a small olive grove. Vassilis and Eleni's father, mother, brothers, and sister were hitting two trees hard and fast; small yellowish-green olives pelted the tarps. One or two people climb the tree to get at branches too high or inside to reach from the ground. A young tree can't support more than one person. Most of the trees in the grove were old.

The stick I used was like a walking stick. You have to swing it hard along the length of the branch. Several of us would work a tree at the same time, one pruning it and the others hitting it. When the olives have been knocked off, you gather them onto one tarp, remove the leaves and twigs, and lift the tarp to pour the olives into large sacks.

In *Rainbow in the Rock: The People of Rural Greece*, Irwin T. Sanders describes how olives are harvested in other areas. In the Ionian Islands, the olives are gathered when they fall. In other areas, people pick the olives they can reach and then use long-handled rakes to "comb" the trees. Vassilis tells me that in some nearby areas in the Peloponnesus the "combing" method is used because hitting the olive trees with sticks damages the trees, making them more susceptible to frostbite.

Eleni's family brought their sheep and goats along to graze on the mountainside. The animals can't be left hungry at home. The family also brought its donkey. The donkey carried the sacks of olives out to the road where a tractor would later pick them up and take them to the plant to be pressed for oil. Eleni and her mother made a bed for Baby by turning the donkey's packsaddle upside down and padding it with blankets.

Eleni's family keeps a portion of the olive oil as its year's supply. The money the family receives for the rest of the oil provides a crucial part of the family's annual income.

Leslie and I had been working about two hours when we all stopped for lunch. We spread cloths under a tree and sat down to a meal Eleni's mother had made in Revmatia and brought down. Fried salted cod, wild greens prepared with herbs, fried zucchini, feta cheese, tomatoes, homemade bread, and homemade wine. It was a sunny day, almost warm. After that terrific lunch we all worked at a furious pace for about three hours.

December 4

From a student composition about winter:

"The people is wearing warm clothes and the children are waiting forward to snow. I like snow and I wish to snow frequently."

December 13

Yesterday Leslie was shopping and met George, an 87-year-old man who lived in the U.S. 50 years. Leslie and I were walking in Meligalas today when she saw George and a woman getting out of a taxi. George introduced us to his wife, Vee. She was going to the dentist, and George offered to buy us coffee.

Chubby and energetic, George looks boyish. He wears a neatly trimmed grey goatee and a dark blue Greek captain's cap. He grew up in Solaki, a tiny village east of Meligalas. When George was 15, his father died from a wound he received in the Balkan Wars. George would have been drafted if he hadn't caught a boat for New York. His brother had gone a few years earlier. George worked with his brother in a confectionery. Then George worked in a restaurant in Philadelphia, moved to Chicago and began a small restaurant, sold it, bought a bigger one, sold that to buy a 24-hour restaurant seating 300 in downtown Chicago.

When George was 33 his brother persuaded him to get married and introduced him to Vee, a 16-year-old with Greek parents. George and Vee ran the restaurant together and sold it when he reached 65. They visited Greece for two years and they both liked it. Twelve years ago they moved to the house where George had been born and remodeled it.

I asked what he liked most about the U.S. "Baseball," he said, grinning. "I always got a season ticket for the White Sox."

Vee returned. She is short and pudgy. Her nervousness is the opposite of George's at-peace-with-himself presence. Leslie and I suggested driving them back to Solaki so they wouldn't have to take a taxi.

Solaki is poorer than Meligalas. At first, Vee invited children to their house to teach them English. She hasn't conducted classes for years because few children live in Solaki now. As with most small villages, the young people move to find work. A few have settled in Meligalas and a few more in Kalamata, but most go to Athens.

In the U.S. their home would be a standard, middle-class house but here it seems palatial. George loves the house and Solaki. Vee wants to move to Kalamata.

"There's nothing to do in Solaki," Vee said, turning to George. "We've got fresh air and quiet," George said.

"The cemetery has the same to offer," Vee replied drily.

December 18

I've given several finals recently. I was surprised at how openly the students cheat. After the tests were handed out, the students began talking to each other about it. I announced that no talking was allowed, patrolled the large room, and smiled at those students who looked around to see where I was. The cheating, assuming it continued, stopped being so obvious. I did not have to make announcements in the other finals.

The other day I spent a few minutes watching from the hall as another teacher (a Greek) gave an exam. She sat at a desk in front of the large room reading a magazine and didn't even look up when students raised their voices and talked to classmates several desks away.

Anna, a pupil I am tutoring, told me a friend of hers advised her to cheat on exams if the proctor seemed like a "good" person (that is, lenient). Anna said Greeks love to cheat, to go around the rules — she gestured with her hand, as if it were a fish swerving in a stream — but that it was a trait she didn't like.

Another student told me about a group of university students who bribed a classmate. The student showed up for a final, then sneaked away with it. He went to his car, which he had parked in front of the building, and began looking up the answers. As soon as he found one, he read it into a microphone. He had placed a loudspeaker on top of his car. (What did other students, taking exams in other rooms, think of the broadcast?) The professor didn't realize what was happening until halfway through the exam.

Christmas

A noon feast at the Zambaras house, prepared by Eleni. Leslie brought over a plate of deviled eggs, which we all gobbled up as quickly as we could. Then we sat down to the main course, lamb with spicy gravy and potatoes in a delicious sauce. Eleni had baked some fantastic homemade bread (only the second time she has made bread), and we drank the Zambaras's homemade wine. Vassilis observed the wine hasn't really "turned" yet, in the wooden barrels out in a small shed in their yard; it tastes like grape juice without the sweetness. A cooked piece of meat on my plate looked like a testicle. I asked Vassilis what it was and he assured me it was a kidney. Without much gusto, I ate it; it tasted fairly good. After I finished it, Vassilis announced it was a testicle. Next, cookies and finally we stopped, all of us sufficiently stuffed.

Baby can almost stand by himself now. After lunch we played with Efiniki and Baby and listened to Christmas music. A sunny day, after a grey, cold, wet couple of months.

Around 3:00 we all drove up to Revmatia, the mountain village where Eleni grew up. At 22, Eleni is the oldest of six children. Her father, born in Revmatia, is a shepherd with his own flock of 35 sheep. He also does construction and seasonal work. Now he is helping people harvest their olive groves. Takis, the oldest son, apprenticed himself to Meni and learned enough to begin doing metalwork on his own. The second oldest son, Theodoros, works as a plumber. The three youngest children still attend school.

Eleni's mother cares for the children, keeps the house clean, does the laundry by hand, cooks, makes the family's bread, cheese, and pasta. Plus, she tends two vegetable gardens, many rabbits, one pig, and takes their several goats out to graze. Sometimes she cards and spins wool. And, like other women in the village, she has a loom.

The family lives in a two story stone house. On the top floor is a kitchen and a large bedroom, which they also use as a living room. The bedroom has two double beds, a big dining table, two cots, and plenty of floor space. They don't have a tv, phone, refrigerator, or hot water. On the bottom floor is a big cellar, where the loom, the homemade wine, the olive oil, the fodder, and other things are stored. And in the yard is a brick outhouse with a toilet, sink, and bathtub.

Soon after we arrived, Vassilis's friends and cousins showed up with shotguns. Vassilis invited me to go with them to hunt thrush, but I don't like hunting. Vassilis left, and a little later Eleni, her mother, Leslie, Efiniki, and I walked around the village making Christmas visits. Both Vassilis's and Eleni's relatives live in Revmatia.

It's a poor village but everyone offers cookies and water along with coffee, a liqueur, or homemade wine to all who visit. "We have the hospitality like something holy," one of my students wrote. Each house we visited had a fireplace in the kitchen, oregano hanging in a clump on a kitchen wall, a single bedroom, and no phone. (The *kaffaneia's* phone serves all of Revmatia.) Only one house had a refrigerator.

As we were walking down a narrow street we saw an old man, one of Vassilis's cousins, in his backyard. He yelled to us, asking Leslie and me if we knew the area code for Mexico. He was waving a bloody and gleaming knife in one hand and in his other hand held a headless rooster upside down. He was disappointed we didn't know the area code and said he had a daughter in Mexico he wanted to call. He hadn't shaved for a few days, his hair was tousled, and he had been drinking. He began to shake his knife at Efiniki and shouted he was going to cut off all her curly hair. He grinned as he made the threat. When he took a step toward her, she ran down the street and hid behind a house.

After a few more visits we returned to Eleni's family's house. Leslie and I sat with the family around the fireplace in the kitchen. They occasionally stirred the tripe soup in a black pot that was suspended over burning branches and glowing embers. We sat there, joking, drinking Eleni's parents' homemade wine (which *had* turned), some cousins visiting for a while, children running in and out playing with balloons, Efiniki trying to sing "Jingle Bells" (she knows a few lines and fakes the rest until the HEY!), everyone eating Eleni's mother's delicious homemade bread, and everyone happy. HEY!

Vassilis returned, after sundown. He had shot three thrush but couldn't find where two of them had fallen. Soon most of us sat at the long table, Leslie and Efiniki the only females among us. Eleni's mother, Eleni, and her younger sister, Angeliki, served us and ate their shares in the kitchen. Leslie wanted to help but was told she couldn't; she was a *guest*.

This second feast of the day began with the tripe soup. Leslie and I were served a single bowl of it, and the tripe lay in the bottom of the bowl in braided strips. Observing Leslie's reluctance to eat it, I told her I'd eat it all for us. After I had dutifully eaten half the tripe Vassilis said not to eat it if I didn't want it. I gratefully gave him a nod and began on the piece of lamb Eleni's mother had served in tomato broth with rice. Everyone also received thick slices from a special Christmas bread decorated with a cross stamped on the top of the loaf.

We had brought a bottle of brandy as a gift. As we left, Eleni's mother gave us a bottle of their homemade wine and half of a big round loaf of her fabulous homemade bread. We have visited Revmatia about eight times now. Eleni's family always treats us with loving kindness.

1984

January 16

From Leslie's letter to her parents and brothers:

We went with Vassilis to an olive oil factory last Friday where his olives were being processed. There are various mechanical methods by which the oil is processed, and this factory had the "old-time" machinery (as opposed to more modern).

First, a description of the factory itself. The room with all the machinery is in an old stone building with plastered walls, the whitewashed plaster chipped away in places where bamboo poles used horizontally as a building material showed through. The machinery was painted green and made a terrible, loud noise. The olives first went through a separator where the leaves & twigs were sucked out by a vacuum pipe. Then they went up into a huge vat where 2 gigantic granite millstones rolled around in a circle, smashing the olives to pulp. The millstones looked to be about 4 ft. high and 2 ft. wide.

Then the pulp was spread by a hand-operated machine onto 3 foot wide circular woven hemp mats. The mats were then piled on top of each other in stacks; these were piled on top of each other to a great height (7 to 8 ft.) and put in the press. A piston came up from the ground to compress the mats together, thus squeezing out the oil & water.

The last part of the process was a "separator," a machine that evaporated the water, leaving pure oil, which poured out into canisters. Above the press was an icon, a drawing in a frame, of St. George, and above the separator an icon of a female saint. These were the very Greek touches of the place!

January 18

I was in my study when I heard a knock on the front door.
When I opened the door I saw the dwarf who lives in a nearby
village. She was walking back out to the street, and I realized
she must have knocked several times before I heard. I called
and she turned, came back with a big bunch of narcissus tied
together with a string. Radiant yellow bouquet. I asked her
how much. Fifty.

She rides a small bicycle. We have smiled at each other in
Meligalas for months but before today never exchanged anything more than standard greetings. I like her, was very happy
to buy something from her. Vassilis told me she makes her
living by selling seasonal things that can be gathered in the
countryside: greens, snails, wild asparagus, flowers.

I wonder if now she will come every once in a while with
something seasonal. That would be nice.

Ten minutes after I typed the above paragraphs there was
another knock. It was her again, and again she had a bunch
of narcissus. She handed it to me, seeming certain I would take
it. And I did. I smiled as I paid. She looked up at me seriously.

January 19

At the Kalamata movie theater today, no line, just shoving
from all directions towards an outside ticket counter. After I
bought tickets I had to force my way back out of the crowd.
It was a crowd of men, the women waiting, like Leslie, at the
edge of the swarm.

After the movie, Leslie and I made the mistake of getting
up along with the rest of the audience. We were moved in a
flow of people crushed against each other. In the lobby, Leslie

said a big man, now in front of us, had elbowed her in the back, hard, to get by her. I hit his back with my palm, hard enough so he would know it was on purpose. He turned. I glared. My retaliation was not only stupid but was not Greek. A Greek would not have taken offense.

January 20

Awakened this morning by a knocking on the front door. It was the dwarf with three bunches of narcissus which she held out to me. I couldn't think of what to say. Leslie and I have been talking about how we are low on money this week. The dwarf looked up silently, continuing to hold the flowers out. I asked her to wait and went to talk with Leslie. We agreed to buy one. The dwarf is serious about her business and didn't smile.

January 21

The dwarf came again today. Leslie and I were in the kitchen. The dwarf must have knocked at the front door a number of times before going around the house, up the back stairs, and across the terrace, to knock at the kitchen door. Now we have four bunches of narcissus.

After she left, I wondered what she thinks. After all, we live in a small house; why would we want four big bunches of narcissus in the space of three days? We put one in my study, one in our bedroom, one in the kitchen, and we took the fourth over to Vassilis's mother for her nameday.

January 22

Woke up this morning to a knocking on the front door. The dwarf had left a bouquet of narcissus at the threshold and was walking away. I took the flowers and walked out to her to hand them back. She refused to take them. She said she had many and pointed to where she'd parked her little bicycle at the corner. Several bunches of narcissus were tied to the metal rack above the back tire.

I said that today we didn't want any. She repeated, in a friendly way, she had many. I walked with her to the corner, trying to think of what else I could say in Greek. "Now we have many and today we don't want any more," I said, "but thank you very much." She smiled and accepted the flowers.

February 1

the village death bells
for a funeral
today

it's possible to ignore the notes,

but almost impossible
not to
pause

as they begin

February 4

I now have several private students. Teaching the twins today. The word "surveyor" is in the text, and I ask if they know what it means. George says no and Andrew says yes. I ask Andrew to explain it. He laughs, says he can't but *knows* what it means. If you know what it means you should be able to explain it, I say. He protests, laughing, then ventures: "If a ship goes under water and only one person comes up, he's a surveyor."

February 11

I scheduled my lesson with the twins this Saturday morning for 7 a.m. so I could get back to Meligalas and drive Leslie and Vassilis's mother up to Revmatia for the slaughter of the pig Eleni's family has been raising. Vassilis said if we got there too late they'd kill the pig without us.

Eleni's mother had built a fire under a large cauldron of water outside. Everyone was wearing winter coats; the day was cloudy and chilly. The men stood together on the concrete porch. The view down the mountain and over to other mountains was magnificent. Leslie and I have sat on this porch many times, often eating delicious foods Eleni's mother prepared. But now someone had taken away the wooden chairs.

Eleni's mother led the huge sow out of the pen. As the sow came down towards us she saw the six men, all visibly excited and nervous, some of them holding knives. The sow began to fight and the men rushed her, pulled her over to the porch, and flipped her on her back. Her legs kicked out with dangerous power, her tongue twisted and extended full length, she screamed with incredible volume, a hoarse bellow more piercing than anything I've ever heard. The men couldn't hold her still and had to dodge her violent kicks. The bellowing continued; the men's cursing sounded feeble in comparison. Efiniki began to wail and was led inside. Finally the men were able to overpower the sow and Eleni's father cut her throat.

Eleni's brother, Theodoros, threw water onto the slit throat to clean the wound of blood; the sow's knee jerked. He did it again and the corpse shuddered. Everyone laughed. Other men started prodding or kicking the body. It had been a hard fight. I think everyone needed relief.

Vassilis told me that last year, when she was less than two years old, Efiniki laughed when they slit the pig's throat. This year her crying lasted a few minutes after the sow's death and then she hurried out. She started hitting the sow's back and laughing.

February 12

From Leslie's letter to her parents and brothers:

Yesterday we went up to Revmatia, Eleni's family's village, to watch the slaughtering of their pig (gruesome, aren't we?). Actually, it was one of those "once-in-a-lifetime" experiences that we thought we'd like to see, a major event in the village life, and something that is a common event in most of the world, though not for us city dwellers. The pig was bought by Zambaras as a piglet last August, and then they shared the expense of the feed and the work of butchering and will share the meat. It was a big sow.

After she was dead, the first task was cleaning the carcass and pouring boiling water over it to loosen the hair, which was then scraped off with a knife. While the men did that, Eleni came out with the jugular vein, fried and cut in pieces, considered to be one of the finest delicacies of the pig. Angeliki brought glasses of wine. Then the pig was cleaned out, after very carefully being opened up. Finally they washed it off again and hung it up by a rope in the middle of the kitchen from a hook in the ceiling. There it was to dry for a day.

All of the pig is eaten, nothing is thrown out. The intestines are used for sausage-making. We had a really excellent lunch of liver and heart cooked in wine, olive oil, lemon, and oregano. At first we were hesitant about eating anything, with the memories of the morning's event still fresh upon our senses, but it was a very good meal, with bread, feta, and wine (*all* homemade & *great*)! Eleni's mother sent home with us a bottle of wine, a loaf of her delicious bread, a hunk of fresh cheese, and some pork. All in all, it was quite an experience. From where John and I were sitting, we stared at the pig during lunch! It took up quite a bit of space in the kitchen, which is small. John and I were the only ones content to leave it alone. Eleni's brothers slapped it now and then, one played it like a drum, someone danced with it a while holding onto the flexed forelegs, and Baby, perched in Eleni's arms, reached up for an ear when Eleni had her back turned, preoccupied with other things.

Today they were going to cut the carcass into pieces and salt it to cure for a week. Next week they'll make sausages and smoke all of the meat.

February 19

The sow screaming, ridged roof of mouth, tongue stretched out, reminded me of the horse in *Guernica*.

March 7

Three sisters live nearby. Annoula, the youngest, just mastered walking. Vasso, almost nine, conducts herself properly and self-consciously. Leah, at seven, is enthusiastic and spontaneous.

At first Vasso and Leah visited together, sometimes bringing a friend (a different one each time). The friend would gawk at what the sisters had probably described before the visit: how the foreigners' house looked inside and what the foreigners themselves looked like up close. And they'd get to hear the foreign man speaking Greek as if it were almost a different language, the words thickened and off-balance. And then the foreign woman who, amazingly, spoke Greek beautifully, though with a limited vocabulary.

After a while the sisters ran out of friends to take inside the foreigners' house. Now only Leah visits.

March 14

Leah Visits our House Again

One of the few
villagers, and the only
child, who understands

for us to
understand
Greek must be slow.

Butterfly
in her drawing

bigger
than a roof.

Her older sister
has other places to go.

You're
welcome

her latest
English

she
awaits
each

Thank you.

March 16

At the farmers' market in the upper square on Saturday morning, Leslie and I were looking at the apples a woman had in a cart. I asked in Greek if they were hard or soft. The woman burst into laughter and then assured me they were hard. Later, Leslie explained I'd asked, "Are they hard or jack offs?" The words for "soft" and "jack off" are identical, except for the accent. You can't listen to most conversations without hearing "jack off" several times, especially if kids are talking.

March 21

As I drove to Kalamata today a priest at the side of the road frantically waved his arms as I approached. I stopped. White beard, white hair, black robe, black hat. He needed to get to a village near Kalamata. He was a thin, old man, about 75.

I asked him to wear the safety belt. He understood my Greek and answered that he wouldn't put it on. Learning that I teach English, he eagerly told me he teaches religion at the high school in Meligalas. He crossed himself each time we passed a church and so was constantly crossing himself.

When I stopped at the village where he wanted to go he reached into his pocket. I smiled and said *No*. He held out a handful of change, and I repeated *No* and thanked him. For the first time he really smiled. He got out of the car, closed the door, and waved.

March 29

Efiniki, who turned three two days ago, was standing by the front gate yesterday, looking out at the street. A stranger walked by.

"Hey, you with the big prick!" Efiniki yelled.

The man turned. "Who?" he said. "*Me?*"

Eleni was in the yard behind Efiniki and didn't have time to do anything but laugh.

A few weeks ago Vassilis's mother taught Efiniki a traditional Greek riddle. The first, second, and fourth lines always remain the same, but the third and fifth are invented by whoever tells the riddle. She taught Efiniki this version:

A: I love you very much.

B: Where do you put me?

A: On the oven.

B: What if I fall off?

A: You have to eat the old woman's cunt.

Vassilis told me that for a day Efiniki walked around Meligalas reciting the riddle. People asked her where she had learned *that*.

"From grandma," she said, thrilled to see their shocked faces.

May 1

From Leslie's letter to her parents and brothers about our Easter in Kalamata and the baptism in Meligalas:

Saturday night at midnight was the celebration of the resurrection of Christ. We went to a church by the sea to watch the service. Fireworks, loud explosive ones, were going off by the dozens in and around the crowd. This tradition originally was meant to scare off the "demons," but now it is obviously tremendous fun for schoolboys. The noise was deafening, and some people were nearly injured and probably burned a little by explosions near bare legs. I've never heard or seen anything like it! No quiet, beautiful fireworks for Greeks — only the loudest satisfy! The beauty of the service was ruined a bit. The service consisted of the priest lighting the people's candles from his, and people lighting each other's candles too, all in total darkness. Then the priest came out and chanted on the steps, and people greeted and kissed each other, saying, "Christos Anesti!" ("Christ is Risen!") And everyone sang an Easter hymn together (which could barely be heard over the explosions!). An old Greek man was swearing about the kids shooting off fireworks during the hymn. Then the church bells began ringing. People walked and drove home trying to protect their candles as it is supposed to be good luck to arrive home without your candle going out. On the way home we saw fires burning effigies of Judas, which had been hung on makeshift gallows the day before, another Greek tradition.

Then Sunday, the big day of the baptism. The baptism was at 4:00 p.m., and Sunday morning we still didn't know what Baby's name would be! It ended up being Tasso, Vassilis's father's name. After all the fuss, Vassilis told Eleni she could pick the name. She wanted Vassilis to discuss it with her so she could choose a name they both liked, but Vassilis refused, saying, "You know what name I want." Anastasios is the whole name, and it means "resurrection." Tasso's nameday is on Easter.

The baptism was amusing since John didn't know what to do, and the priest had to demonstrate rather than tell John what to do. At one point John had to blow in all directions, then spit in all four directions, and everyone laughed as the priest demonstrated and John mimicked him. Baby screamed when they undressed him, and he peed all over the place. Poor Baby was scared to death! Then John and Mary (godmother) had to oil Baby, *every* nook and cranny: teeth, ears, between toes, etc. He hated it and was crying hysterically. Then, plop, into the huge cauldron of the baptismal font for total immersion. He didn't like that either! Then finally out, dried off, and into the new suit of clothes John had bought him. Then John, Mary, and the priest, John holding the baby, circled the font a few times, and it was over. Baby regressed to infanthood in his terror and sucked his fingers the rest of the day, something he hasn't done since he was 6 months old!

The party after the baptism back at the Zambaras house was fantastic! There was roast lamb, 4 salads, sausages, bread, ouzo, and wine. The Greeks, however, hardly ate at all but sang the whole time! For more than an hour the whole room sang old Greek folk songs. One old guy, Vassilis's first cousin (son of Vassilis's father's brother), drank quite a bit of wine, led the singing, and at one point stood up on the bench he was sitting on and danced! After about two hours we all went outside on the patio to dance.

May 9

taped to the green
fuel tank of the
shepherd's motor

bike a
photo from
some magazine
of two women

kissing, and on
his seat a
lamb skin, not to
mention the

tall green stick, spring's
stalk, he
wedged

stands
straight
up

from the
handle

bars

May 12

I'd met Jenny months ago in a musty shop across from the Meligalas post office. Jenny and the old lady who owns the shop are about the same age and keep each other company. The pair asks me prying questions whenever I go in to buy a notebook or pen. How much rent do I pay? How much am I paid in Kalamata? Why don't Leslie and I have children? How much did my car cost? As my Greek has improved they have asked nosey questions about the Zambaras family too. I answer questions about me but with questions about the Zambaras family, I usually pretend I don't understand. The two raise their eyebrows skeptically and try repeating the questions. I know how to say, "None of your business," in Greek now but prefer using what seems to me a politer method of warding them off.

Jenny asked me to go to her home and address some envelopes to a son in the U.S. Today Leslie and I walked to her house. Jenny was expecting us and, although we were early, was waiting at the door. Pale, white-haired, thin, she dresses in old black clothes. Her living room was dusty, cluttered, with framed black-and-white photos hanging on the walls and standing on tables, a rectangular cracked mirror (held together by its wooden frame) hanging from a nail on a wall, clothes heaped on chairs and in corners, and in the middle of a round table a fluted glass pitcher stuffed with letters and slips of paper. There was a smell in the house I couldn't identify, and Leslie told me later that it was rancid oil.

After we addressed about two dozen envelopes to one of her sons, which she said would be a year's supply, she served us remarkably stale cookies from a pink box with large oil stains on its cardboard sides and bottom. She had probably bought the cookies from the Meligalas bakery, anticipating more Easter visitors than had come. She told us about her family, pointing to the framed photos and handing us the smaller ones. Then she showed us a photo of a chubby woman, grim and homely and standing awkwardly with her arms by her side. The woman was in a new black dress. "I was pretty then," she said proudly, standing near us as we looked at the photo. The photo was taken soon after her husband had died, when she was 40 and her sons were four and nine.

She took her sons to the U.S. but because of visa problems she could only stay three years. Both sons live in the U.S. now. Jenny became sad, thinking of them so far away, and began repeating sorrowfully that someday she would die alone and no one would care.

May 15

The day before yesterday we went to visit George and Vee. They weren't home. As we were getting into our car to leave, one of their neighbors appeared and told us that George went into the Kalamata hospital two weeks ago because he had pneumonia. We visited him last night. He looked fairly good. He said on May Day he had been watching tv in the afternoon and got up to go to the bathroom. In the bathroom he began to sweat, felt as if he were immersed in water, and then his shoulders, back, and chest started "killing" him. He said it was like being crushed by an octopus. Leslie told me later that what he described sounded like a heart attack.

Vee called a doctor and he told her to get George to the hospital immediately. They've been at the hospital since then. George's room has three beds; an old man occupies the bed at the foot of George's bed, and Vee has been sleeping in the empty bed across from the old man's bed. Many patients have a relative or friend staying with them because the nurses do little except distribute pills.

Two nights ago George had a heart attack. Vee doesn't understand what a heart attack is and knows nothing about the pills the nurses bring a few times a day. She has asked the nurses for information, but they won't explain the pills or anything else. It's impossible to know what they *could* explain; they don't get much training.

Once a day the doctor rushes from bed to bed, ordering Vee out of the room when he looks at George and then saying almost nothing to George. When he passes Vee in the hall he refuses to speak to her. George says if she visited his office in the hospital the doctor would talk to her. Vee says that the couple of times she has gone to his office she has seen a big group of people waiting to talk to him and that he ignores you unless you slip him money. PASOK made bribery in state hospitals illegal, but it is unlikely anyone would dare to report his or her own doctor.

May 21

The doctor knows about George's diabetes but hasn't ordered a special diet for him. Every morning George has been served chocolate pudding, the standard hospital breakfast. Leslie's nursing training has been helpful. George and Vee thought the doctor wanted George to eat the pudding and the desserts that come with other meals. Four days ago Leslie convinced them there could be no reason to prescribe such food for a diabetic.

Leslie and I both really love George. We have been visiting him daily. I take her to the hospital on my way to work.

Sometimes I can see George before classes begin, and I've been visiting every night after school. Leslie often stays seven or eight hours and drives home with me or sometimes she stays five hours and catches a train home.

Now all three beds in George's room are occupied. At night Vee sleeps in a chair near George's bed. The new patient, an alcoholic, was brought in because he had a heart attack. For the first few days, he was in great pain and swore continually. Vee was shocked.

The first time I heard Greeks swearing was on a visit in 1982. I was helping Vassilis with some construction work that he and Eleni's family were doing. There were many excited outbursts. When I asked Vassilis to translate, he told me the last two remarks had been "fuck your god" and "fuck your Virgin Mary." Apparently, Vee hasn't heard these standard Greek curses before. She told Leslie that the alcoholic was swearing against God. "That's blasphemy," Vee said. "Isn't that blasphemy?"

The day the alcoholic arrived the doctor connected him to a portable heart monitor. The nurses and doctors never even glance at the monitor. Nevertheless, the patient, pale and weak a few days ago, looks much better now. He has stopped cursing. This afternoon, while Leslie was there and each of the three patients had a group of visitors, he suddenly said loudly, "Look at that!" He smiled and pointed at his monitor. "My heart's like a ship." He touched one of the peaks on the graph. "There's the smokestack, and it's going over the waves. No, it's mountains and trees. Look at all those tall trees. My heart is full of trees because I come from a village with lots of trees."

May 22

Last night the patient across the hall from George, a farmer, deliriously chanted that the hay was high and his donkey should keep moving. This morning he began again. A nurse told visitors in another room and led them to his open door. The nurse and visitors stood there, laughing.

May 25

Yesterday Vee arranged to visit the doctor at his other office. Today I drove Vee to the shabby building. A narrow hallway led to his metal door. We rang the buzzer and he opened the door, frowning. We followed him through a tiny, empty waiting room into his office. He went behind his wooden desk and gestured for us to sit in the dusty chairs in front of the desk.

Vee opened her purse. His expression changed from indifference to something like a smile. He expected to be paid. Vee took a folded piece of paper out of the purse with the questions that we had helped her prepare. The doctor grimaced. We had guessed he wouldn't give us much time, and so we limited the questions to five and arranged them from most important to least. The first dealt with what Vee should do for George when he returns home. The second asked the doctor to identify the pills George is being given. We also wrote a preface, telling the doctor to avoid technical language because Vee doesn't understand it.

As he spoke I looked at the bookshelf behind him. The dust covering the books and magazines showed he hadn't consulted them recently. On top of the bookshelf was a glass case, its contents semiobscured by dust. Two skinny stuffed birds stood inside the case.

The doctor answered Vee curtly. After she asked the third question, he gave a deliberate look at his wristwatch. His reply lasted eight or ten words, and then he said he was busy and we had to leave. Vee opened her purse again and, as before, his face brightened. Vee handed him cash. He led us through the empty waiting room to the door. In the hallway, Vee told me she didn't understand most of what he said because he failed to use layman's terms.

May 30

Vassilis says Meligalas is buzzing with a story Mrs. Fotopoulos told Saturday. She said she was walking by our house when she heard Leslie and I scream. Seeing we were terrified of a snake in our front yard, she yelled, "It's not poisonous." But we went into our house, locked the door, and stayed inside for hours. She shouted to us, after we'd locked ourselves in, "Why don't you kill it?" We answered, "We don't kill snakes where we come from." The Saturday morning she said this had happened was a morning we had left early to go to the beach. Not only had she made up the story, she also invented a custom for us.

When she sees Leslie (usually at least once a day), she always asks where Leslie is walking to or from, what Leslie has cooked or will cook for each meal of the day, where we went if our car had been gone for part of the day. It hadn't occurred to us she would tell other villagers the news, but it seems she does. On Saturday our car was gone before she had a chance to question either of us. Without a news bulletin her role as investigative reporter had been denied her, and on a *Saturday*.

Vassilis had showed me a front-page story in a local paper last week: a man in a nearby village opened his car's hood to work on his engine and found a big snake curled on top of the air filter. Maybe this tale inspired her.

June 3

I was driving back to Meligalas. As I rounded a curve a man walked onto the freeway and raised his hand. His thumb was missing. Another man down the road stopped cars coming the opposite direction. I looked for an accident but saw no cars on the stretch they were blocking off. The man yelled to me, "Half a minute, half a minute!"

Soon many cars had lined up behind me. I was looking at them in my rearview mirror when something exploded behind a low hill nearby. My car shook and big rocks sailed towards me. Three landed about 15 ft. away. They were bigger than footballs, easily big enough to smash through a car roof. I couldn't help laughing, it seemed so Greek. It would have been too much bother for the man to walk another 30 ft. and stop us farther up the road, where it would be safe.

A second BOOM and more rocks shot up from behind the hill to thud near the road. A third blast but no rocks. The man walked off the freeway and casually, with the thumbless hand, waved us on.

June 9

George has been home for a week. He feels much better. Vee has been talking about his grave. It has been embarrassing to listen to her talk about it in front of him, as if he had died in the hospital. Today, she took us into the kitchen so George wouldn't hear and demanded that we go to the Meligalas cemetery and pick out a tombstone design for him. We asked why *we* should pick it, and she said because Leslie has "an artist's eye" and I'm "sensitive." We protested that she and George should choose the design but she begged. We gave in. She immediately commanded Leslie to bring her a sketch of the design.

We arrived a little before dusk. Almost all of the newer marble monuments and headstones are gaudy. We finally found an elegant, modest design. As Leslie began to sketch, I walked toward the black wrought iron fence. A tractor approached on the one lane road, pulling a cart full of hay and followed by a flock of 80 to 90 sheep. The man driving didn't look over at the cemetery. Two boys sitting on the front edge of the cart didn't look over either but crossed themselves as they passed. The sunset dyed the round backs of the sheep deep orange.

June 11

the widows
in black
are at night

yelling to
each other over
the dirt road
on which they live

separately

voices of complaint
dispute
lower
for gossip

the full moon

sometimes a laugh
usually not joined

dogs from all directions
yap

one woman sighs as if shifting
some burden
they speak
with such energy breaking

the silence breaking it
into pieces as small
as stars

July 4

Nightmare last night: I was in bed at night and woke as I was lifted by two big arms, one grabbing me between the legs and the other around the neck, like I was an animal. I knew I was going to be killed, stabbed, and was helpless, could only scream, bellowing, and realizing in the horror of it that I sounded just like a pig about to be knifed, and that made it even worse.

The most horrible part of it was *being* a scream, all of me a terrible bellow of fright and protest, as if that would save me though at the same time I knew it could not.

July 15

Leah sees us on the street and brags she has been to the beach nine times this summer. She groans, as if learning of a death, to hear of our four.

Then, later today, the man in the Meligalas hardware store asks us if we have been going to the beaches. Not as often as we'd like, Leslie says. THERE IS (he declares, raising his hands) NO MORE (shaking both hands at us) BEAUTIFUL (pause) BEACH (with one hand he caresses an imaginary horizon or maybe it's an expanse of sand) THAN THE GREEK (long pause) BEACH. ONE MUST SWIM (another shake of the hands) IN THE MORNING (he looks into my face seriously and then into Leslie's) AND (longest pause yet) AFTERNOON.

I explain that we haven't been able to go to the beach as much as we want because I teach in the mornings and after-noons even though it's summer. He says he hasn't been able to get to the beach as much as he wants because he has to stay in the store.

July 16

Between private lessons I drove to a little park to eat a sandwich. After lunch I realized I'd locked my keys in the car. One front window was slightly open.

I went to the *kaffaneia* opposite the park, and its owner (about 60) led me to a building under construction next to his shop. He bent down, grabbed part of the thick wire fence, and broke off a wavy length about 2 ft. long. Then I followed him to a nearby auto repair shop. We walked to the back and he put the wire in a vise and straightened it. A young mechanic wandered over. The older man bent a hook at the bottom of the wire. The mechanic asked what he was doing.

"My friend locked his keys in his car."

I was touched by how he said this.

He handed me the wire, saying, "Well, this should do it," smiled, and stayed to chat with the mechanic.

A boy and a tall, fat man stood beside the car. The fat man had poked a stick through the window. I watched him fail, and then I tried the piece of wire. I couldn't position it to catch the lock knob. The fat man took the wire out of my hand, bent the hook into a much larger semicircle, put the wire through, and caught the window handle. After I thanked the man and boy, they strolled over to the *kaffaneia*.

I returned to the *kaffaneia,* wanting to buy drinks for the fat man, boy and owner; as I hesitated, trying to figure out how to say this politely in Greek, the owner and the boy got into a small pickup truck. The owner leaned out, told me to sit, and said to the fat man, "Give him whatever he wants!"

July 17

George

not

that he doesn't love
Jesus, worked
in a church after
he retired

and when he started to paint
bought a color-by-number
Jesus.

But the two purple irises
and seven yellow daffodils
in a white bowl

he painted by himself, and on
a larger canvas. Each

daffodil bell

a shade of green the
yellow stamen
stands out in

in the living room.

Jesus
waits in the back room, on the blue wall
with icons.

July 17

I've occasionally discussed Germans with my students. Many German tourists visit Kalamata each summer. The students say they feel no bitterness about the war but then observe resentfully that Germans feel superior to Greeks. The students complain that the Germans act very coldly.

Last night the man at the Meligalas hardware store began talking about Germans. He hates them because they killed so many Greeks during the war. They rounded up 2,000 partisans and machine-gunned them in Kalamata. He pretended to be machine-gunning, to make sure Leslie and I understood. In a small village nearby they killed 80. They killed his brother.

July 18

Driving into Meligalas tonight, 8:15, still light, and in front of the new, trendy *kaffaneia* a young man (20?) in a pressed, white long-sleeved shirt stood in the road, his back to my approaching car. He was fashionably dressed, like the other young men sitting at the sidewalk tables. He raised his arm and pitched something. I saw a Gypsy boy, about eight years old, his shirt and shorts both a dirty grey. He ran and I realized the man had thrown a coin. The boy was now bending to look in the gutter, which was filthy with dirt and trash. Unable to find the coin, he stepped forward to look again.

Note

Between 100,000 and 250,000 Gypsies live in Greece, about 1-3% of the Greek population. They are Greek citizens, with all the rights of citizenship. Many Gypsies live in a suburb of Athens. There are also many nomadic Gypsies in Greece. I've often seen groups of Gypsies living in tents set up in olive groves near Meligalas. Some of the men are peddlers or migrant farm workers. Others trade and sell livestock, especially horses and sheep.

August 30

From Leslie's letter to her parents:

Tuesday evening we went by Vassilis & Eleni's and found that they were all in Kalamata at the hospital because Eleni's mother fell out of a fig tree on her back, and Angeliki told us (Angeliki was at the house with Tasso) that Eleni's mother couldn't walk or move her head. We worried all Tuesday night, but Vassilis came over Wednesday a.m. (yesterday) and assured us that she hadn't broken anything but hit her shoulder on a rock and was in great pain.

Yesterday we went to the hospital with Eleni and Angeliki. Eleni's mother was in a lot of pain but was getting better. She could move her head & neck again (her legs were only a problem right after the accident because of shock). She was very unhappy to be in the hospital. Vassilis said she may have to stay another week. That is probably good, since she will go right back to work when she gets home.

After the hospital, we took Eleni up to the mountain village to do some work her mother normally does. Did we get a taste of how hard her mother's life is! We went to the two gardens that she works, one on the road to the village, the other a mile and a half steep downhill in a little river gorge in the mountains behind the village. It is a beautiful spot and a great walk *down*hill, but coming back is a killer.

The garden is quite big, rows of corn, tomatoes, eggplant, zucchini, beans, peppers, and probably a few other things I didn't notice. It is by the river, and they have made a little irrigation ditch to the garden. The river comes down a rocky gorge, and a spring rushing out of the rocks is one of its sources. We picked a bag of beans and filled a big basket with tomatoes and eggplant. That was heavy going up the hill back home! Thank goodness, Theodoros (Eleni's brother) rescued us on his motorbike by hauling the stuff halfway back.

On the way we saw in the distance on the hills a man on a donkey, leading another donkey and herding goats. He was singing loudly. Eleni told us the man is 85 years old, takes the goats out every day, and is always singing!

Back at the village house the chickens had to be fed, and Eleni fed the goat with branches of foliage she'd chopped off on the way back from the garden. Also, the pig had to be fed, and we picked figs and corn from the fields behind the pig's shed and saw the tree Eleni's mother fell from. Eleni cleaned the house up, in disarray since Sunday when the accident happened, and tried to talk Theodoros into eating something besides tomato salad. That's what Eleni's father & brothers had been eating, since Eleni's mother does the cooking. ALL of these things, trips to the garden twice a day, as well, are done by Eleni's mother alone. I don't know how she finds time to make their bread, cheese, pasta, etc., and even weave (not to mention shearing and spinning the wool to yarn). It is no wonder she looks so old for her age.

August 31

In the Meligalas hardware store the young wife is watching her younger-looking husband talk with the owner. The husband says, quietly but deliberately, he has seen gas burners *just like this one* in Athens, and much cheaper. The owner doesn't look at him but at the burner; he spits on the rag in his hand and wipes grime from the enamelled white. The boy speaks with disgust of the price, the owner continues rubbing the burner, and the wife's eyes rove over all the goods.

September 1

This afternoon Leslie and I were walking in Meligalas. We saw a thin, elderly man walking towards us. We didn't know him, but as we usually do with everyone in the village, we greeted him. He returned our greetings. He was carrying a galvanized pail with an old checkered cloth covering its contents.

After we passed, the man called us. He had stopped. He called again, looking at me. I walked over, wondering what he wanted. He reached into the pail, brought out several small green figs and held them out, with a smile. I thanked him and took the figs, and then, carefully, he selected two more. I thanked him again and we said goodbye.

Last January we drove to Koroni, a fishing village. On our way we took a wrong turn and got lost on a small dirt road up in the mountains near Kalamata. We saw a shepherdess with a few sheep on a slope near the road. We stopped and I got out to ask directions to Koroni. She said to keep going. We did, and reached a dead end about three minutes later. As we returned I worried she might be annoyed with us for coming back so soon. Had she misunderstood my question? She was standing at the roadside, apparently waiting to talk with us. I stopped and she reached in through the open window and placed in my hand a handful of walnuts and almonds.

A few weeks ago an older couple was camped out near their drying currants so they could cover them if it rained. We stopped the car to take a picture. As Leslie talked with them they became friendlier and friendlier, giving us first a few bunches of currants and then seven small green pears. They only had twice that many pears and had brought them to the field (where they were staying all day) to serve as part of their meals.

September 23

Drove to Athens to meet the poet Robert Lax, who lives on Patmos but was in Athens for a few days. We met in our hotel lobby. About 70, Bob is a tall, thin man with a big, wonderfully long face, deep-set blue eyes, and greyish-white, short hair. His full, rounded goatee gives even more length to his face. It is difficult to think of him without thinking of him smiling. He said he knew a good cheap place for lunch, if we didn't mind a walk. It was about 40 blocks away, and Bob seemed like he could walk all day with the same lively step. He came to Greece in 1963. He said when he got here he wrote pieces he'd always wanted to write while living in New York. But then he looked around, saw how the Greeks were living, and began writing about them. He said Patmos is like Delphi: "At both places, the tourists move through like smoke."

During lunch we talked about Thomas Merton (whom Bob had known since college), painters, religion, Lao Tzu, Greece, Paris, Bob's favorite writers (Rabelais, Joyce, and Beckett), and jazz. He told of being introduced to a jazz musician by a friend who said, "This is Bob. He lives on an island." "I carry my island with me," the musician replied. Bob said he loves that idea. "Bob is a poet," Bob's friend added. "Oh, that's a great line," the musician said. "I use it sometimes too. People want me to do something, and I tell them *Don't bother me, I'm a poet.*"

Bob walked back with us to our hotel, and we arranged to meet at his hotel later. Outside his small hotel that evening, we saw him sitting inside on the narrow, white marble lobby steps, knees together, head bowed, looking like a shy boy. The evening darkened as we walked to another restaurant which, like the place where we'd eaten lunch, was cheap, distant, and had no tourists besides us in it. As we walked we talked about travelling. He asked if we'd been to Zagrev. I wasn't even sure where it was. Yugoslavia. He said it's the darkest place he has ever been. "At night, it's like night coming to night."

September 27

The first color postcard of Meligalas arrived yesterday. Printed in Athens, photographed and sold by Thanassis, who runs a sort of anything-and-everything shop which has the village's only copy machine, the village's only Polaroid for passport photos, postcards on wall racks and revolving stands, plus costume jewelry, stationery, cassettes and records of Greek music, glass animals, stuffed animals, decorations for whichever holiday is next, computer games, lighters featuring naked young women, key chains with raised individual Greek letters on oddly shaped pieces of metal, Fuji film, Kodak film, novelties like bird-headed devices that keep dipping in and out of a glass of water, and secondhand souvenirs from around the world, including a wooden-handled glass beer mug from a bar in the U.S.

The new postcard shows three antiseptic, deserted scenes. The photo on the left is of a paved street. The houses to each side of the street have been newly whitewashed; small in the distance, at the end of the street rises the hill with the church on top of it. Not even a leaf in the street, or a bird anywhere. The right side of the card is halved: a photo of the upper square with its recently painted church is above a photo of the train station with its new stone facade.

September 30

Vassilis told me a story about Nikos, a cousin of his from Revmatia who has lived in Athens for more than 10 years now. I know Nikos, a smart, robust, burly man with a fine sense of humor. He has made a good living by his wits, selling a variety of modern goods. Recently he has been selling and installing home alarm systems.

On a visit to Revmatia Nikos suddenly became very sick. His family couldn't figure out why, nor could Nikos. A cousin of his in Revmatia, an old woman, asked if he remembered anyone giving him the evil eye. Nikos didn't believe in the evil eye, but he did remember someone in Revmatia giving him a spiteful look. The old woman prepared an herbal broth. After Nikos drank it he recovered immediately.

October 1

Sunday morning. Outside the Revmatia *kaffaneia* a priest, who lives in a nearby village and performs services there as well as in Revmatia, is sitting with three young men. The priest has coffee and two of the men are drinking ouzo. Vassilis, Leslie, and I arrive. The priest calls us over and insists on paying for our order: two small Greek coffees and an ouzo for Vassilis.

The priest is 35 but his lean face has deep lines. Vassilis, who usually despises priests and describes them as greedy parasites, tells us this priest is an exceptionally good man and a Communist, a rare political affiliation for a priest (at least in this area). Vassilis says he asked him how he reconciles his politics with his religion and the priest answered that Christ was a Communist.

A farmer walks by carrying fresh walnuts and gives us some. As we talk we crack them open on the concrete floor. Villagers pass on the narrow, winding road. Autumn is coming. A man driving a tractor is pulling a cart heaped with grapes, and someone takes some bunches for us. Sunday morning, a wonderful slowness and leisure. We sit there, in the sun, for more than two hours.

October 6

(going by on train)

and a road
stretches a moment
into a village

October 9

We woke up last night at about 4:30. Little bits of plaster from the roof were falling on us and all over the bedroom. Leslie thought it was an animal up on the roof, and I thought it was an earthquake. At 6:30 this morning, a larger earthquake shook the house. It is 2:45 p.m. and there have been four more quakes since then, all relatively small. They seem small enough so that there's no real danger. But, of course, what do I know?

Now it is 10:30 p.m. Tonight, in class, my students said that 80 stone houses collapsed in a nearby village. There has been one more big quake since I wrote the paragraph above and about four more smaller ones. Someone said a donkey near his house began braying at 4 a.m., half an hour before the first quake. Another person said a dog in a neighbor's apartment started barking at 3 a.m.

October 15

At 8:15 this morning I saw the fishseller's little blue pickup truck driving through Meligalas. I was walking back from the post office, and he was heading into the square. He was holding a microphone and announcing his fish for sale as he drove slowly. He stopped talking and started to sing a Greek folk song in a wonderfully corny way. I looked back and saw people standing still, listening. After he sang for half a minute he quit and drove silently by his smiling audience.

From Leslie's letter to her parents and brothers:

Well, George is back in the hospital, this time after a stroke. We didn't find out until four days after it happened, then it took another day just to find him in the hospital building despite a search by John and telephone calls by Vassilis. Five days was enough time to do damage before I arrived and told Vee they *must* turn George every 2 to 3 hours to avoid bedsores and exercise the paralyzed joints or the joints will freeze. That is *basic*, *basic* nursing care, but nothing was done and his joints are stiff (not frozen, thank goodness) and worst of all, his buttocks have terrible sores.

George is very depressed and won't open his eyes or speak unless provoked. Actually, it is good for him to get his anger out. He refused to respond for an hour and a half while John and I were there today and finally opened his eyes and said angrily he wanted to get up and walk, the doctor said he should, why wouldn't we get him up?

About the walking, yesterday some shit of a doctor looked in the door and shouted, "Get him out of bed and walking today!" He yelled this at Vee and me. George is a big man, and when he hadn't even sat up in bed once, with one side paralyzed, the doctor wanted the two of us to get him out of bed and walk him??! Your sense of balance is altered with paralysis so I suggested that we sit George on the side of the bed to let him get used to it and ask the physical therapist about walking tomorrow. George can't even keep himself upright sitting on the side of the bed. It is so frustrating to see him neglected in the hospital.

November 6

Vee took George home from the hospital yesterday. We promised we'd visit this morning.

When we knock, Vee opens the door. She says George is in the bathroom. In a few minutes he walks slowly into the living room, using a four-legged aluminum cane, and sits in a chair near the window.

"Baseball on tv last night," he says.

"When we lived in Chicago you used to go to the ballpark to see our team play," Vee says. "*Our* team. What was its name?"

George stares at her silently.

"Remember *our* team, George?" She stands and walks over to him. "You used to love to see them play. What was their name?"

"White Sox."

"That's right, honey. Now, what was the name of the other baseball team we had?"

Silence. George looks out the window.

"The other baseball team," she demands. "What was *its* name?"

He continues looking out at the yard.

"Honey, honey, are you there?" She shakes a finger in front of his face. "What was the name of the other team in Chicago?"

"Cubs," he mutters.

"That's right. Now, what was the number of our house? Remember, our first house? It had a little red roof. What was the number of that house?"

George stares out the window.

"The number of our house." She bends to talk into his ear. "What was the number of our house? Remember? In black numbers, you nailed it up yourself, those black metal numbers over our white door. That nice white door. You used to paint it every year."

George begins to shake. He cries.

"That's all right, dear," Vee says soothingly. She puts her arm around him. "Don't cry. Don't you remember the number of our house? One hundred and twenty-eight. Don't you remember you said you hoped we'd both live that long? One hundred and twenty-eight."

George says the number sadly.

The phone rings. Vee picks it up. "Costas," she screams. "Sweetheart. How are you?" She loudly tells Costas, a cousin in San Francisco, how rough the two weeks have been on her: the bad food in the hospital, the nurses did nothing, she couldn't sleep at night with all the worry. And why didn't Costas call sooner?

After talking to Costas for five minutes, Vee says George would like to talk with him. She thrusts the phone at George menacingly. "Talk to him," she says in a stage whisper. She tries to put the phone in his hand, but he refuses to hold it. "Talk to him," she orders. "It's Costas, your cousin."

George doesn't move, refusing to even acknowledge he hears her. Vee pushes the phone into his hand, bends his fingers around it, and tries to make him lift it.

"Don't resist me," she threatens.

George waits for her to let go of his hand. Then, with difficulty, he raises the phone. "Hello," he says faintly, then drops the phone without waiting for an answer.

"Talk to him!" Vee says. "Ask him how Jane is, and the kids. C'mon, George, you've got to talk to him. Say *How is Jane? And the kids?*" She begins to force the phone back up to his ear. Although he fights back, she overpowers him.

66

"Hello, Costas," he says softly. Then he cries with big, heaving breaths.

"Ask him about Jane!" Vee commands.

"How Jane?" George says, sobbing. He drops the phone. Vee grabs it and starts to say something to Costas, but apparently Costas interrupts, says goodbye, and hangs up.

"Costas had the nerve to bawl me out," she says angrily to Leslie and me, "for not letting HIM know George was in the hospital. Who does he think he is? Don't I have enough problems on my hands?"

November 9

Visit with George and Vee. George asks if we saw the Syrian dancers on tv last night. I arrived home too late from teaching, but Leslie saw them and says, "Weren't they great?"

"They dance as if they're electrified, like they're being poked by cattle prods," Vee says. "I told George to look at those feet, that he has two feet just like them."

George begins tapping both of his feet. We all laugh, and George, laughing, keeps tapping his feet. His health improves daily.

November 10

    they're following the

    sunshine around

    the porch

                  our cats

    Leslie's words

December 9

On the 7th, Leslie and I took a train to Athens. She flew to Arizona this morning and will be there six weeks. I rode the train back to Meligalas.

December 10

The manager at the supermarket, in his early 30s, asked if I am alone now. (Leslie had told him she was going to the U.S. for a while.) I said yes.

"That's better."

Not knowing what to say, all I could do was smile with surprise. He didn't seem to be joking. Before I could think of a reply he walked away.

He has been married for a year or two. His wife's family owns the supermarket.

A minute later I knew what I wanted to say. And I could have said it in two words in Greek. "I don't think so."

December 17

George returned to the hospital a few days ago because of heart problems. I've been visiting daily. Today he looked a strange pinkish-yellow and breathed with difficulty.

"Do you know what happened?" Vee asked urgently. "The man across the hall was supposed to go home to Athens today. His family lives there. The doctor promised him he could leave this morning. He got dressed, he was walking up and down the hall, he was all ready to go." Vee paused dramatically.

"He was all dressed, was happy, his wife was with him, and he was telling everybody he'd be home for Christmas. Then the doctor came and told him he had to stay a few more days, for more tests. The man said he'd leave, tests or no tests. The doctor ordered him to stay. Then the doctor went back down to his office. A minute later the man's wife screamed and I thought, *Did she see a snake? Did she see a mouse?* It was a horrible scream and so I ran over. She screamed because she saw her husband's eyes roll back up into his skull. He was dead! I'll never forget it. The doctor came and said nothing could've been done for him. It was tragic. He was 55."

Vee suddenly screamed, imitating the woman's scream. George winced and closed his eyes. "Only 55," Vee said. I thought of my age, 33, and how long I may have to live. "Only 55," Vee repeated. George, 87, lying in bed, kept his eyes shut.

December 23

The First Words on the Small
Village Train Station

in thick black Greek
pencilled
large on the fresh peach

colored
wall

GOOD MORNING

JACK OFFS

December 24

George is home again. Weak, but happy to be home. Vee had Christmas cookies today, and there was an old lady in black there whom I have never met before, a neighbor, and we were all joking around. The old lady laughed with her mouth nearly shut and talked that way too. It was only after a joke she thought was really funny that she couldn't help laughing with her mouth open, and then I saw she had no teeth.

Walking to Vassilis's tonight and seeing flickering lights in an upper story window. It was a Christmas tree. A little farther along I saw a second blinking tree at a window. There were no flashing trees last year.

A year of change in Meligalas. The first color postcard of the village, most of the last dirt roads now paved, two new modern supermarkets opened, a Meligalas hospital clinic nearing completion, and blinking Christmas trees. But not all change is desirable. For example, the sign in English for travellers leaving Meligalas announces CAME AGAIN. I suspect that within a decade someone will change it to the forgettable COME AGAIN.

December 31

This morning the first carolers for St. Basil's Day arrived at 6:20. I had gone to the bank to get a lot of coins. Usually only children make the rounds, but at about 7:00 I opened the door and saw the dwarf woman accompanied by two girls who were about 13. The dwarf stood in the middle and sang as loudly as the girls but, unlike the girls, didn't smile as she sang, though she looked right into my eyes and her eyes twinkled.

A little later a boy squeezed by me as I opened the front door. He ran through the open door of the bedroom. As he sang he darted looks around the room at the unmade bed, the long brick and board bookshelf jammed with books, books scattered on the floor, chair, bed, and especially at the framed paintings of Leslie's on the walls, some of them female nudes. It was as if he had entered a Martian spaceship; he couldn't look around enough. At the end of his song he grinned triumphantly. He'd get not only coins but a good story. I asked him his age. 11.

Leah and Vasso came about fifteen minutes after it seemed that no more carolers would arrive because it was getting too late. I invited them into my study. Vasso began playing one of those plastic mouth pianos with black and white keys. She wasn't playing a tune but more a sort of tribute to being able to move fingers up and down, up and down, depressing the keys. What emerged sounded Turkish, and Leah sang along heartily while tinging a miniature triangle.

1985

January 2

Ran over, through a drizzle, to the bakery. To keep the loaf dry I put it under my coat and held it. As I walked through the street I felt its warmth against my chest. Hugging it, carrying it home in an embrace.

January 4

Today I was in Kalamata and went into the hardware store. Tommy, Bob's younger brother, was behind the counter. I forget who said "Happy New Year" first. We smiled. Then he looked at me strangely, as if wondering something.

"You heard about Harry, didn't you?"

I must have looked confused.

"My brother," he explained.

"Oh, you mean Bob?" I knew him as Bob. His family had lived in Boston for years. Bob and I would speak in English, just as I also spoke English with Tommy.

"Yes, Bob. He died a month ago. He had a heart attack, went to the hospital, and the next day he was gone."

Tommy told me that Bob was 43. He said Bob had been planning to get married later this year to an American woman who lives in the U.S. She had visited him last year.

When Bob saw me enter his shop he would always call out my name and smile. Last year he helped me buy a wedding band. He knew Leslie and I were only engaged. I explained it might be good to wear a ring so people in Meligalas would think we were married. (After I began wearing it, Mrs. Fotopoulos told everyone that Leslie and I had recently gotten married in Kalamata.)

Bob suggested that I buy the ring from a friend's shop. He went with me and was patient when I was indecisive. I asked if he thought the ring I was considering would seem an appropriate width. He replied that I shouldn't care what people think.

Bob negotiated a low price for the ring. As we left, I asked if I could buy him a coffee. He said he had to return to work. And now I remember how he said he had no time to go to the beach last summer, not even once; one of his assistants hadn't worked out, and he'd had to fire him and do the extra work himself.

It was his first heart attack. Tommy said it was so sudden that Bob didn't know what was happening.

January 5

A cold morning. I buy a magazine from the man in the kiosk in the lower square. I've bought magazines from him twice before. I've never said more than good morning or good afternoon to him. As he gives me the magazine today he says, "So you're alone now?" It seems everyone in Meligalas knows.

"Yes, but my wife returns on the twentieth."

He smiles and, sitting in the little space inside the kiosk, lowers his arms to his waist. Then he says something I don't understand, except the word "cold." Perhaps something about catching a cold, or eating cold food, or some unusual comment about the weather. Or, most likely, from the way he grins, some sexual reference such as, "don't let the equipment get cold." He means it as a friendly joke and laughs at his own wit. I laugh along with him and, seeing me begin to laugh, he really laughs hard. A warm moment, no matter what the joke might have been.

January 21

Yesterday I met Leslie at the Athens airport. We took the train and got back to Meligalas last night. This morning Vassilis drove us to the Kalamata customs office. We had left our car with customs because it is registered in Leslie's name. She has a tourist visa while I have working papers; we pay less tax with the car in her name.

Upstairs in the office we are given an application form to fill out, and then an official needs to rubber-stamp the application, a second official has to register some facts in a big notebook, a third must stamp it to show the facts have been recorded, a fourth needs to figure out how much must be paid for storage, a fifth across the hall has to okay the fee, a sixth at the cash register has wandered off and we wait five minutes for him to return. When we pay he tells us to go to another desk. Forty-five minutes after we began ricocheting between officials, the paperwork is completed.

An official sends us downstairs to a man in his 50s at a desk in a warehouse. He has the keys for all the cars in the yard. We tell him ours is a Peugeot. He asks when we brought it in. December. He opens an enormous record book to look up the entry showing when the car came into the yard, confident he'll locate it immediately, but soon he looks puzzled. Someone else logged the car in six weeks ago; the other man must not have recorded it, he concludes. He grumbles, gets up, says he must go into the next building and upstairs to see his superior.

As he is walking out Leslie says he wasn't even looking at December. He had the notebook open to the last days of September. Vassilis turns the pages to December, and he and Leslie quickly find where the car was entered. Vassilis goes to fetch the man.

The man returns. He nods, as if the fact that the entry was found in his absence was to be expected. He opens a bottom drawer of his desk, takes out a package of Marlboro cigarettes that has something written on it. He shakes his head, reaches down and brings up a Camels box, and reads the scrawl on that.

One by one he brings up different used cigarette boxes. He lays them across his desk in three long rows. A man stands in the warehouse doorway grinning, obviously finding the scene comical. He calls out he has a truck in the yard, and the official tells him to wait a minute.

The official opens a box and pours out a pair of keys. Not ours. Bewildered, he asks for our car's make as if for the first time. He begins replacing the boxes in the bottom drawer, one at a time, rereading the scribbles. He pauses, holding one and staring at it, then looks up, questioningly says *Peugeot* and when we all nod, he half-heartedly smiles.

We go out with the key as the official begins talking with the other man. Our car is between a smashed taxi (front totally crunched) and an old red Mercedes: six inches to move forward, eight to move back. The three of us return to the warehouse. Vassilis asks the official if the Mercedes behind us can be moved.

"Easy," he replies. Another official has appeared, a man in his early 30s. This official is ordered to get the Mercedes's license plate number. He walks out with us, reads the number aloud, and walks away.

It seems we don't need Vassilis as a translator now, and he goes home. Eleni was expecting him half an hour ago.

Leslie and I get into our car to warm it up. We sit in it five minutes, the engine idling. We had assumed the official would return with the Mercedes's keys to move the car. I get out of our car wondering what happened and spot the man on the far side of the yard opposite the warehouse. He's chatting with a janitor. When he sees me he waves, nods, and strides toward the warehouse.

After sitting in the car another few minutes, I go back into the warehouse. The first official is still talking with the trucker. The official asks what I want. I say the Mercedes hasn't been moved. He asks for its license number. I don't know what it is. He decides he should go out and get the number.

When we return to the office all the cigarette boxes re-surface to be ploddingly put into rows again. Again, no key. He rereads each box, placing them slowly, singly, back into the drawer. There are many different packages, a few repeats (four Marlboro, three Camels) but most of them unique, and several brands I've never heard of. Back out they come. He finds the key and calls over an official who was standing, almost hidden, behind a stack of boxes. Our official gives the key to the other official, telling him to move the car.

This man, in his early 60s, glances at me morosely. I'm the reason he is being forced to do something. He doesn't seem to want to budge, so I walk in front of him. He follows with small steps like a four-year-old. I get into our car and he tries to open the Mercedes door. It won't open.

He begins cursing the car loudly, then yells to me. I can't open the door either. He shuffles to the passenger side. That door is jammed too. After a couple of minutes he succeeds in opening it. The Mercedes is close to a car beside it, and the man can't squeeze in the partly opened door. I get in and try starting the motor. Nothing.

The official from behind the warehouse desk shows up, curious why the older official didn't return. He manages to get in the Mercedes but can't start it. He puts it in neutral. The two officials and I push. The car is immovable. We guess the emergency brake must be on, and I get back into the car but don't see it. Leslie says she might be able to find it. In a few seconds she locates it.

The younger official says he'll steer while the older man and I push. The car moves an inch. And now we notice the rear tires are up against a bump in the asphalt. It takes four efforts, the older man and I straining, for me to figure out we need the other man's help. He glumly gets out of the car and Leslie takes his place. The three of us shove the car a foot. And that's enough.

January 23

While Leslie was gone, Mrs. Fotopoulos's daughter, Yiota, got married. We saw her today, in front of our house. She excitedly asked Leslie, "How are you? How was your time away? How does John seem to you now? Did he stay healthy while you were gone?" After answering her questions, Leslie asked where Yiota is living. She and Petros are renting a house on the other side of Meligalas. "A nice house," Yiota said, smiling. After describing their house she asked what Leslie was cooking today.

"Beans," Leslie said. "Me too," Yiota said happily. "I'm cooking beans today." Then Yiota shrugged and trying to look serious she raised her hands and said, "What can we do?" (In other words, what else can we afford?) Yiota couldn't suppress a smile. She looks very happy.

Whenever Yiota's mother sees Leslie she asks what Leslie is cooking. This is the first time Yiota has asked.

January 28

A cold grey morning. My neighbor Roula is walking the path by my study window. I have the overhead light bulb on, and it shows through the thin, blue curtain. She probably knows I'm here and wants to find out if she can see me through the curtain. She slows and casually turns her face this way, as if glancing at the house for no reason. Almost immediately she looks straight ahead again and quickens her step. It's not that I wanted to watch her. But I was thinking, and she walked into the scene. I knew she was going to look in. And when I pass her house and her door is open, I look in.

February 1

The word *chaos* was in our book. I said, "That word's from Greek, isn't it?" One student said it in Greek and several repeated it, enjoying how it sounded so different from how I'd said it.

A student raised his hand. "Chaos is our world," he said, cheerfully. "It's the Greek world."

I laughed and agreed. On second thought, I asked him to repeat what he'd said.

"It's a Greek word."

"Ohhhh. You know, I thought you'd said *It's the Greek* WORLD. And I agreed."

All the students laughed.

"You know, the trains aren't on time here, etc., etc." I gestured, the way a Greek might, to imply a tumbling, accumulating chaos.

"Yes," the student said, laughing. "That's right."

February 3

We had dinner last night with the newlyweds, Yiota and Petros. Petros grew up in a village near Meligalas. He is a Communist and moved to Germany in 1967 to avoid imprisonment when the dictatorship came into power. He lived there five years. He's 40 and Yiota is 22. He works at a Meligalas warehouse; five hours a day of loading and unloading sacks of fertilizer.

Leslie and I volunteered to help with dinner. Yiota said only Leslie could help because we couldn't all fit into the kitchen. I stayed in the central room with Petros. In one corner, his table with a lamp where he studies current events and economics after Yiota goes to bed. And in another corner, their bed. He took out a pearwood recorder and said he taught himself to play in Germany. His big hands have large knuckles and square-tipped fingers. He played Greek folk songs and stopped after each to explain the lyrics, careful in his choice of words because of my limited Greek.

Petros proudly repeated several times during the night that to be a Communist means you study (the words for "read" and "study" are identical in Greek). It wasn't pride in his own intellectual pursuits but simply a statement that he has found a way to live that satisfies him.

Five months ago, during a period when the warehouse laid him off, he got work plastering a house across from ours. Leslie and I remembered seeing him and a man he was working with and hearing them sing together when they took breaks. Petros said that was when he met Yiota. She brought them water, coffee, and oranges. He laughed, implying one thing led to another.

February 5

Near our house, an olive grove on a slope facing west, *the* place I felt one with the hills and valley and nearby mountains, a place I hated to think of leaving. Although the grove is close to Meligalas, a hill behind the grove blocks off noise. And I've never seen anyone there, though sometimes I've heard sheep bells nearby.

This week, at the foot of the slope, a bulldozer gouged a gigantic rectangular pit for the new dump. Dead turtles lay scattered among the upturned clods of dirt. Understandable to locate the dump there because much of the nearby countryside has something profitable growing on it while this plot had been covered by grass, shrubs, weeds, and asphodel.

It's easier now to think about leaving.

February 10

Yesterday, in Olympia, Leslie and I were walking around slowly, looking at items in an enormous tourist shop. The only other person in the shop was the clerk, a boy about 18, the same age as many of the gods on vases, coffee mugs, key chains, plates, trivets, ashtrays. He sat at a desk near the door watching an old black-and-white cowboy movie on a large tv. He had turned the volume low; subtitles provided words.

Leslie and I examined the souvenirs, and the boy, trusting we wouldn't pocket anything, stayed in the Wild West where there was a woman, a man who loved her, and villains to be killed.

February 15

almond blossoms
in grey
dusk
appear
as if their tree
weren't there

February 17

One of the Meligalas taxi drivers died a few days ago. A burly, big-bellied, fierce-looking man, probably about 60. Had a flat tire, lost control, and crashed into a ditch. He didn't think he had been hurt seriously until the next day. Then he went into the hospital. They discovered internal bleeding, sent him to an Athens hospital, and he died a day or two later.

He had a forbidding look, and that, plus his fascist politics, had made me avoid him. However, two months ago Leslie and I walked over to George and Vee's and then it started to rain. Vee called a taxi for us and he drove over. We talked during the ride, and since then we would greet each other. When we passed on the road, going opposite directions, we'd wave.

In the village many people have their place, or places, and are seen there a number of times a week. The taxi driver liked to sit at one of the outside tables of a sweetshop in the upper square. When I walk by the sweetshop and see the empty chair at that empty table, I can almost see him there, facing the street, looking surly, and then waving.

February 19

In Hills between Villages

With a shovel, the man down there
in a black

smoking field of fallen and standing
stalks. A single blank glance

to our passing train.

February 25

Clean Monday

First day of Lent, the day
kites are flown.

9 a.m. I open my shutters &
feeling the wind,
look at the blue for kites.

None, but the old widow
across the street
has just let out

her chickens.

At 10:20 a few shapes
gliding
in spirals

pigeons,
taking off from a church on the hill

no one in sight
holding their strings.

February 26

From Leslie's letter to her parents and brothers:

Monday was the first day of Lent, and we went to the village of Messini for their Carnival parade. We wandered around a while and then sat down at a sunny table in front of a coffee shop, sheltered from the cold wind. We drank coffee, and then ouzo, and by that time we saw we had some of the best seats in the village, right on the street where the parade would pass, and in view of the stage where the dances would be performed. It also was one of the warmest spots in town!

The parade came right by us, children in costumes, five "floats," and the Messini marching band (an interesting combination of 10 instruments, played by embarrassed-looking adolescents).

The floats were funny. One was a big, cylindrical man with a head that turned, one a multicolored cannon with two military men next to it, one a funeral scene of a young man who died of too much "eroticism" and a "priest" presiding, waving a pornographic magazine to the crowd as evidence. Another float depicted the "parity of the drachma to the dollar" with a giant one drach coin and a tiny dollar bill. And there was a strange flower-bedecked one with homely little girls all dressed up in beautiful dresses. A fun element was that most of the floats from Messini and other nearby farming villages were pulled by tractors.

My favorite part of the parade was a mock wedding scene, which according to my readings is a tradition for Clean Monday festivities, though the wedding takes many different humorous forms. This wedding had a very small, beaming old guy for the bridegroom and a 7 foot giant of a man dressed in drag as the bride. It was funny!

The rest of the festival consisted of folk dances on the big stage in the square. During all of this, firecrackers were going off, and confetti was floating down to the streets from the balconies.

April 2

A few days ago I played backgammon with Christos, my landlord's brother-in-law, who is in his mid-70s. We played in a *kaffaneia* in the upper square. A thin, old man next to Christos was soberly following each move. Vassilis said Christos was once the best player in Meligalas. I expected to lose.

As we began I had luck. A few rolls of the dice later, he moved his pieces farther than his roll allowed. I mentioned this. He looked surprised, apologized for the mistake and corrected it. I had more luck. Then he made another move that was better than his roll permitted. After I said something, he again looked surprised and then apologized and fixed the move. His third such move occurred as I was about to win. His surprise was not convincing.

I won, 3-2, pure luck. After the first game Christos didn't make any more "mistakes." I asked Vassilis about that game. He said Christos had been testing me. If I was stupid enough to be cheated, why not beat me that way?

April 4

Vassilis said that Greeks are much more impressed by Easter than by Christmas because "anyone can be born, but it's something else again to be resurrected."

May 26

Visit with George and Vee. Vee said she wished they lived in Athens. George said he didn't like Athens. "After Chicago," Vee pronounced, dramatically, "Athens is," pause, "a thumbnail," longer pause, giving each of us a look, "of nothing." I laughed and said I wanted to write that down.

"Write it down! Write it down!" Vee said. We were sitting out on the porch, and she abruptly got up and went inside. She came back with a big piece of white cardboard on which something was written in ballpoint pen. She handed it to me. The title was "Thank You, God, For The Gift of Life." I read it and handed it to Leslie. "Read it aloud," Vee insisted.

Leslie read it aloud. Then Vee said George had written it. George had been smiling and sobbing silently, as Leslie read it. I wondered if he was remembering when he wrote it. It was dated almost 20 years ago to the day.

"He had been working so hard," Vee said. "When he retired, then he had time to think. He started painting. And little by little he wrote sentences, things he thought of, and I told him he should put them all together on a page, and he said he didn't want to. But I said they should all be together in one place, and that's what this is."

George smiled.

I asked if I could copy it.

"Yes, and put it in one of your books," George said.

Thank You, God, For The Gift of Life

Thank you, God, for this life on earth.

Thank you for its challenges, its excitement, its rewards and its happiness.

Thank you also for its frustrations, its heartbreaks and its disappointments.

As to the future, please give me more of the same if you can. I do not mean to indicate a lack of belief in the next existence after this earthly life is finished.

It is just that I cannot believe it will be much different, so long as it means being alive. We probably will continue to build our own individual hells and heavens.

Perhaps there is an after-life where there will be no problems and therefore no challenges, where we all will be much wiser and therefore much more aware.

Anyway, thank you for the ability to feel and to think, for the capacity to be bold or afraid, happy or distressed.

Thank you for the gift of life.

June 3

From Leslie's letter to her parents and brothers:

Eleni's family had the exhumation ceremony for her grand-
parents. It is amazing to me that that particular custom hasn't
disappeared; it is so gruesome. Eleni and Vassilis said that it
was a very unpleasant experience because Eleni's grandfather,
though buried 10 years ago, wasn't completely decomposed.
The Greeks (outside of the family) interpret that to mean that
the person was very bad. The actual reason was that Eleni's
grandmother was buried under the ground, and the grandfather was buried above her in one of those marble coffin-like
boxes that they build here over graves. They decided to bury
the grandfather for another 10 years, though the priest told
them to go ahead with the ceremony of breaking apart the
bones and putting oil and wine on them.

Note

Vassilis says in other parts of Greece the fact a person's body doesn't decompose
may mean the man was a saint or had a saintly character. Yet another meaning could
be that the person may become a vampire.

In Loring Danforth's book, The Death Rituals Of Rural Greece, he says there
are varying customs as to how long a person must spend "in the ground" before
exhumation. He writes of a villager's exhumation:

> She would be exhumed because her family wanted to see her for the last
> time and because she should not have to bear the weight of the earth on her chest
> for eternity. She would be exhumed so that she could see once more the light of the
> sun.

Danforth observes that the bones are deposited in the village ossuary and that
"the ossuary itself is a powerful symbol of the ultimate unity of the village dead."

June 18

The first time we visited Koroni, a nearby fishing village, was in January 1984. At the pier we saw a crowd. We joined them around a man who was poking in the water with something like a long-handled trident except it had about six barbed tines instead of three. We looked into the water at a big octopus on mossy rocks. The man stabbed it to hold it down. A boy lowered a chunk of something blue on a string, positioning it near the octopus, where it dissolved and made the octopus almost stop moving. Another boy dropped a large three-pronged hook on a line, hooked the octopus, and the man and boy carefully, hesitantly, pulled up the octopus. There must have been about 35 of us watching this happen.

The octopus, on concrete now, looked even bigger than it had underwater. It was a mottled brown, purple, and orange, luminous, gorgeous. Its head stretched and changed shape as it tried to crawl away. The man who had brought it up had moved back into the crowd, as if he too wanted to admire the octopus. Then he stepped forward, lifted the octopus, carried it down the pier, and dropped it on the concrete. He picked up a piece of wood and slammed it against the octopus. We all hurriedly left; no one wanted to see that.

On that 1984 visit it was the size of the octopus that drew the crowd. On this visit we saw small ones caught. A man with a trident-like tool would walk up and down the pier, occasionally see an octopus, stab it, and bring it up. The man would give it to a boy and then continue hunting while the boy threw the octopus down against the concrete. Throwing an octopus against a hard surface tenderizes the octopus. The boy threw one octopus more than 100 times; he was sweating and tired by the time he finished. The huge octopus would have been difficult, if not impossible, to throw.

June 25

Leslie and I were walking to the upper square. "Big, ripe, delicious watermelons," announced a Gypsy over his sound system; he crept towards us in a red pickup truck on a deserted street to our left. A tall, massive, good-looking girl came out her door and, without glancing at the Gypsy, began walking in front of his slowly moving truck. She was wearing a light blue skirt with a lighter blue blouse and looked voluptuous. The Gypsy interrupted himself and announced, slowly and with feeling, "a. . .BIG. . .doll."

The girl kept walking and he followed, once again praising the watermelons.

June 30

It takes two minutes to drive from Meligalas to the little village of Neohori. Last night Vassilis, Eleni, Leslie, and I went to the Neohori panigyri. (A panigyri is a festival held for any one of a number of occasions, usually religious.) We arrived at 10:45, before almost everyone else. The tables were in the street and four musicians were playing on a high, wooden platform.

The bouzouki player sat beneath a bare bulb hanging from a wire. From where we sat we could see his legs, lap, the bouzouki, and part of his chest; the light bulb was so near his head that his head looked like grey mist.

The clarinetist, a thin man with wavy hair combed straight back, played clearly, with strength and unexpected shrieks. He also sang. Vassilis remarked that his deep voice seemed to belong to a man who weighed 500 pounds.

The youngest musician, the drummer, played with the least enthusiasm. A heavy, black-haired man, with his black shirt open to his navel, he routinely marked time.

The woman in the band, 45 or a little older, wore a low-cut, red dress. She was plump, with dyed yellow hair in bangs, and she acted as bored as the drummer. But when more villagers arrived she woke up. When the villagers offered money to the musicians in return for playing a favorite song, they would speak to her and she would lean down, treating the audience to a view of large, very white breasts.

The band had big amplifiers, and I had to almost shout to talk with Vassilis even though he sat next to me. I asked him to translate one of the songs. The words repeated over a dozen times: "My love, I'm going to have a tragic finale, give me some wine, I want to burn in your fire. . . ." For a little variation, he would burn in her fire before he asked for the wine.

By midnight about 300 people had filled the square. Between 10 and 30 were dancing at any time. Sometimes a man would dance by himself, arms outstretched, head down. The dance reminded me of a child pretending to be an airplane dreamily circling the land.

Several young men, when dancing with each other, lifted their arms and moved their bodies in waves as if abandoning themselves to desire. But when one of these same men danced with a woman, his dance was conventional and formal.

July

Visit with Robert Lax on Patmos

In the morning Bob, Leslie, and I walked to a small beach to go swimming. Damianos, a fisherman, joined us. A solidly built, handsome man, about 55, with graying hair and a weathered face, he (like Bob) is gentle and modest. He doesn't talk much and smiles easily, warmly.

Two young couples sat near us, and Damianos knew from their accents they were from Athens. Damianos remarked to Bob he dislikes Athenians who visit Patmos and prefers foreigners. Bob explained Athenians treat Patmians in the hotels and restaurants like servants and regard all Patmians as yokels.

Bob told a story about travelling with a friend. They would bark at each other and have long conversations of barks. Bob barked a few times for me, happy, energetic, friendly barks. On train rides, when the trains passed through tunnels, Bob and his friend would bark loudly to each other. Once they were in a compartment with only one other person, a Japanese man, and when they went through a tunnel, Bob and his friend barked. As they left the tunnel, the Japanese man said, "You know very well how to bark."

Later, when he and his friend were back in the U.S. and living in different cities, his friend would call Bob long distance, and they'd bark for a few minutes and then hang up.

One morning Leslie, Bob, and I walked to the little pier where Damianos keeps his small fishing boat. Damianos had invited us on a day trip to an isolated beach.

We passed an island, a jutting, rocky hill with a small chapel. Bob said Damianos visits the little chapels on barren islands and cleans them once a year. Everyone else has forgotten about them.

On one stretch of beach on Patmos, Bob pointed to a house and said it had belonged to "Captain Tromeros" ("Captain Terrible"), a notorious German officer who lived there during the German occupation.

Bob told us Captain Tromeros had come to Patmos with a 19-year-old Greek boy from another island who was his lover and who also spied for him. The captain shot and killed people in the street, sometimes because he didn't like the way they looked and sometimes because he had been told they were working against the Germans. He had many informers reporting to him.

One day some islanders went to his house. He knew they had come to murder him but had no opportunity to get help. The islanders, the captain, and the boy drank all afternoon. In the evening, when the captain was drunk, the islanders tied up both him and the boy and put them on a boat. Then an islander shot them. Some of the islanders were upset because the boy had pleaded for his life, saying he had been taken by force from his island and had then been forced to act as an informer. Bob says the islanders still argue about whether the boy should have been shot.

Once Bob had taken a boat to another island. He had a snack near the pier. He looked up and saw the boat about to leave. He began to walk towards it. He said he felt like running, but it was as if a hand on his forehead restrained him.

When he got there, some sailors reached out and helped him aboard. The passengers and crew cheered and gathered around him. He felt happy and everyone was congratulating him, saying they'd seen a lot of people run and miss the boat, but he'd *walked* and made it!

He realized later that if the captain saw someone run towards the boat as it began to leave, he would take it as a challenge and pull away fast.

July 13

From Leslie's letter to her parents and brothers:

Damianos is a very nice man, and Bob told us an interesting story about him. At one time, Damianos was very sick with stomach problems, which the doctor thought were extremely serious. One night Damianos had a dream in which his old Aunt Evdokia came up to him and put her hand on his stomach, and his pain went away. He woke up, and the pain was really gone. The doctor examined him and thought it truly miraculous! So Damianos planned and saved for a chapel to honor St. Evdokia, a saint from Patmos, whom half the Patmian women are named after. He did build the chapel, finally, after many dreams in which his old aunt told him exactly where to build it. We visited the chapel, and it is gorgeous, full of hand-painted icons of the saints. Bob says that Damianos goes every morning up to his chapel to light incense and say prayers before the icons.

July 26

(Back in Meligalas.)

Two mornings ago I cleared the weeds from the outside edge of our front wall. I cut most of them down and threw them into the side yard. My neighbor Roula was walking by as I finished, and she declared she would help. She had a shovel and attacked a small patch of ground that had a few remaining weeds. I told her it wasn't necessary, but she scraped the weeds away as if the neighborhood depended on it. (Given the state of the neighborhood, that seems unlikely.)

Having completely destroyed those weeds, she darted into our front yard and raised an accusing finger at a tall bush. I said we liked that bush. She marched over to it and began hacking at a branch that was as thick as a garden hose. She looked at me defiantly as she was hacking away at it. How much longer are we going to be here, I wondered to myself; what's the difference? As if I could have stopped her anyway, short of pinning her arms behind her back and lifting her out of the yard. I went over to help, putting my foot on the branch to hold it down while she slammed the shovel into it.

Deciding that speed was no longer top priority since I had obviously chickened out, she excused herself, walked to her house, and returned with a little axe. After that, the bush was gone in two minutes.

While she was getting the axe, I had taken the branch she had cut and thrown it down into the side yard. After she finished slaughtering the bush, I began to gather the branches and carried an armful toward the side yard. She grabbed them away from me, amazed at my stupidity. "Garden," she shouted, "*garden*!" She dragged the branches across the road, over to her house. Later, I asked Vassilis what she would do with them. He guessed she would use them for fodder or as part of a fence.

July 29

From Leslie's letter to her parents and brothers:

The big event around here this week is the "Garbage Lectures," as we call them. With the awful heat and hot wind occasionally, we've noticed terrible garbage smells wafting in through our windows. It's too hot to shut the windows, but some days we did because of the smell. One morning, after our 6 a.m. walk, I noticed a horrible smell by our front door but nowhere else and then discovered a pile of compost-like garbage thrown next to the house under our bedroom window. It was the kind of stuff, rotten fruit and vegetables with chicken droppings mixed in, that Roula often throws there. She thinks no one is watching her, but I see her from the studio window.

We asked Vassilis to come over and politely ask Roula please not to throw garbage in that particular place, because of the terrible smell. Vassilis and John went to her and very politely expressed this. Roula became hysterical! *She* would *never* do something like that. She's a human being, not a dog! And besides, she gets the smell at her house too, she said. People come and do that at night when no one can see them, she told us. We accuse her when just the other day she helped John pull weeds! She never dumps there, or even closeby, but way down from our house, she claimed.

Well, her whole family (visiting from Germany) came out to assert her innocence. We didn't see her dump that garbage, so who knows? Though I have seen her dozens of times, when she thought no one was looking, dumping trash there (she always looked around furtively afterwards, too!). Anyway, I think we achieved our purpose! *She* certainly won't be dumping there again before we leave; if she isn't the culprit, I think she'll be on the lookout for the real dumper, and neighborhood talk over this should keep anyone from doing it again before we go, so as not to be caught. Every day now, when we see Roula, she gives us an angry lecture (anger not at us but at the mystery dumper) beginning, "Who is dumping garbage there?"!

August 15

The assignment for the twins was to write a story beginning with this sentence: "Not many cats talk, but I do." George wrote:

"It was a Monday morning when I first understood that I can talk like a man. I tried to speak like a cat but I couldn't. I was worrying a lot, I was feeling like a man."

August 17

When we tell people we're going back to the U.S., almost everyone asks why. The first few times, I talked about how we love Greece but love the U.S. too and our families are there. That explanation, simple enough in Greek, tempted Greek friends and acquaintances to dream up difficult questions. I still struggle to say anything complex in Greek and so, mostly out of laziness, I began saying we were leaving because our parents live in the U.S. Until today, that provoked no follow-up questions.

Today, a teenage boy from Meligalas was on the train coming back into the village from Kalamata. We talked about the trade school he attends in Kalamata. He is taking a two-year program which will teach him to be a train mechanic.

We got off the train together, and as we walked up the road toward Meligalas, I told him Leslie and I were leaving soon. He looked surprised and asked why.

After he heard my answer, he was silent for a few moments as we continued up toward the village.

"Why don't you bring your parents here?"

I said Leslie's father and mine have jobs they like in the U.S., and all their friends are there. And Leslie has two brothers, and so do I, and they live in the U.S. too.

"But you love Meligalas?"

"Yes."

"Then bring them all here."

August 20

We wanted to stay in our house until August 27 and travel in northern Greece for two weeks before we left. But we found out that the permit for our car says we are only allowed to have it in Greece for two years with normal taxes on it, and after that there is a daily fine of about $50 a day. We have been in Greece more than two years now.

This provision has been on the car's papers from the day we got here, in small print. Vassilis noticed it two days ago.

Now, we are rushing to get out of the country with the car. One problem is that Greek money is not desirable outside of Greece. We want to figure out exactly how much the fine will be so we can pay it and leave the country with very few drachmas. But the vague provision for the fine gives the customs officials discretion. Vassilis called the Kalamata customs people for us, and they said the fine could not be decided in advance.

In the last three days we have been doing all the things we thought we would have nine days to do: saying goodbyes, mailing boxes of books back to the U.S., cleaning our house so we get our deposit back, dividing up big possessions (mattress, refrigerator, table, chairs, two-burner hotplate, etc.), and little ones (straw hats, snorkels, broom, pillows, etc.) between Eleni's parents and Vassilis and Eleni. Most of it will go to Vassilis and Eleni, but we will give our refrigerator to Eleni's parents, who insist on giving us a large rug in return.

August 21

Arrived in Patras in the afternoon, chose a hotel, then drove to the pier to buy tickets for the boat to Ancona tomorrow. We waited in a long line of cars, and when we bought the tickets we asked how we could determine the fine. The official selling the tickets told us we needed to go to the customs office across town. He gave us directions.

We found the building easily, only to have an official there look at me with disgust when I asked about the fine. He said we had to go to the customs office at the pier where we'd bought the ticket because only *those* customs officials could figure out the fine. We drove back to the pier customs office and the office was empty. After 15 minutes an official appeared and said he couldn't determine the amount until we were actually leaving. It didn't matter if we had our tickets as proof of when we were leaving; he would not determine the fine until the day of departure. I explained I didn't want to *pay* it today but just wanted to know how much it would be. "We can't know," he said, "until you leave."

I have the drachmas for what should be the amount of the fine and for the hotel tonight and dinner. The rest of my money is in U.S. traveller's checks.

The best thing about the day: we found a quiet little bar across from our hotel and played a few games of backgammon.

After the hot day and the frustration, the bar felt like Heaven. A pleasant woman, maybe in her late 20s, stood behind the bar and a few men sat at the tables. The Gypsy music on the tape player wasn't full blast, the overhead fans cooled us, and the sea across the street looked spectacular out the big front windows.

August 22

Our boat was scheduled to leave at 11:30. We arrived before 8:00, and it turns out the customs people don't begin work early. An official told us to return at 10:00.

We found a hotel on the beach and had breakfast in its empty restaurant, looking out at the sea. Then we walked on the beach. More trash floated in the water here than at the beaches near Meligalas.

We played it safe and exchanged more money at the bank, which opened at 10. Got to the customs office, which was about eight blocks from the bank, at 10:18. Waited in a short line. Then it was our turn and the official, when he saw the papers for the car, looked at us with annoyance. He would have to do some thinking on this one. He yelled something. Another official came out from a back room with almost a smile but soon became grim.

The two of them inspected our papers. It was 10:45. They agreed they didn't know how to calculate the fine. One said he would go get the books. He disappeared, returning with a big ledger and two Marlboro cigarette cartons. The cartons were stuffed with pamphlets and forms. The two men started their calculations, obviously confused. It became clear they would charge us more than what I had expected.

We watched the cars driving up the ferry's ramp. One of the officials said it would be about $85 more than what I had figured, $25 more than what I had in drachmas. I asked if they would take a traveller's check. No. It was 11:06. They said we should catch the next boat, in a few days. At which time the fine would be higher, of course. We said we wanted to leave today. They looked disappointed because that meant they still had to do the paperwork. They hadn't finished figuring out the amount and began quarreling with each other about it. Meanwhile, a Greek family had entered the room and stood behind us, scowling at us and the officials.

I asked Leslie to wait while I ran to the bank. And I did run, about eight blocks, and then waited in line behind two people. The line moved slowly. When I got to a window, the clerk was kind and sped up when I told her about the ferry. I exchanged another $50 and sprinted back to the customs office, racing around people on the sidewalk. People coming the opposite way stared at me as I ran towards them. I'm sure I looked like a madman; I felt like a madman.

It was 11:25. The ferry was blowing its whistle, and the officials were talking with the Greek family that had been waiting behind us. Leslie said the officials had told her to step aside so they could help the family, even though they had not completed figuring out our fine.

The officials finished with the family at 11:28. They told us the boat would leave any minute and that they had *almost* finished working out the fine but needed to talk to their boss about it. One of the men strolled away, and the other man looked at us with a combination of boredom and hostility. Outside, the cars and trucks were no longer driving up into the ferry. Sailors were doing last-minute chores on the pier. Unfortunately, there was one more customs window to pass, a small booth, before we could board the boat.

At 11:32 the other official returned. The fine had been determined. I paid, we hurried out to our car, and drove it to the booth. The official in there, his back to the window, was sitting at a little desk. A radio was on and he held a newspaper. I greeted him loudly enough so that he would hear me over the radio but not loudly enough to sound demanding. The ferry blew its whistle. I made an effort not to say anything more; he knew we were there.

After a long minute, he stood, stretched, and took the step to the booth's window. He examined our ticket, then studied the receipt for the fine we'd just paid. He scratched his head, asked a few questions, and leisurely printed our answers onto a little form. As he was writing I asked Leslie to get into the car and start the motor. The official was moving his lips as he read the small form to himself. He nodded, looked up at me expressionlessly, looked down at the form and picked it up, almost handed it to me but changed his mind. He pulled it back toward himself and held it up about eight inches from his face, scanning it to make sure it was perfect. After this final inspection, he handed me the little masterpiece.

Leslie drove us up into the ferry, and 20 seconds later the ramp was removed. Less than one minute after we had boarded we were sailing away.

Standing on the deck, watching the sea widen between us and Greece, we laughed. If the officials had been efficient and we had stood on the deck for half an hour or more, looking at Patras and thinking of our two years in Meligalas, we would have felt sad to be leaving.

John Levy was born in 1951. He grew up in Phoenix, Arizona. In the first half of the 1970s he was a Contributing Editor to *Madrona*, a poetry magazine published in Seattle. After graduating from Oberlin College in Ohio, John moved to Kyoto, Japan for a year and a half in the mid-1970s, where he taught English as a second language. He then moved to Paris, where he lived for a little over a year, supporting himself with odd jobs. In 1980 he moved to Tucson, Arizona and worked as a carpenter and estimator in a small construction company. When John returned to Tucson after two years in Greece, he rejoined the construction company. In 1986 he married Leslie Buchanan and in 1988 he began law school. He is currently practicing law in Tucson.

In 1980 Elizabeth Press (New Rochelle, N.Y.) published *Among the Consonants*, a collection of his poems. John is currently completing a second collection of poetry. A group of his poems appears in *How the Net Is Gripped: a selection of contemporary American poetry*, an anthology published by Stride (Devon, England, 1992) and edited by Rupert Loydell and David Miller. The anthology also includes poetry by Vassilis Zambaras and Robert Lax.

This is an edition of 1,000 copies, 84 of which have been numbered and signed by John Levy and Leslie Buchanan. The book is printed by McNaughton & Gunn, Inc. (U.S.A.). The typeface is Sabon, created by the German typographer Jan Tschichold (1902-1974) in the 1960s.

Leslie Buchanan

51/84